Discovering SAS® Viya®

Special Collection

Foreword by
Randy Guard

sas.com/books

Table of Contents

Free SAS® e-Books: Special Collection

In this series, we have carefully curated a collection of papers that introduces and provides context to the various areas of analytics. Topics covered illustrate the power of SAS solutions that are available as tools for data analysis, highlighting a variety of commonly used techniques.

Discover more free SAS e-books!
support.sas.com/freesasbooks

sas.com/books
for additional books and resources.

THE POWER TO KNOW®

About This Book

What Does This Collection Cover?

SAS® Viya™ is the latest enhancement of the SAS platform. It is designed to address the new, and increasingly diverse, needs of organizations with methods, access, and deployment that scale to meet burgeoning analytics use cases.

To illustrate the power and flexibility of SAS Viya, several groundbreaking papers have been carefully selected from recent SAS Global Forum presentations to introduce you to the topics and to let you sample what each has to offer.

The following papers are excerpts from the SAS Global Users Group *Proceedings*. For more SUGI and SAS Global Forum *Proceedings*, visit the online versions of the *Proceedings*.

For many more helpful resources, please visit support.sas.com and sas.com/books.

We Want to Hear from You

SAS Press books are written *by* SAS users *for* SAS users. We welcome your participation in their development and your feedback on SAS Press books that you are using. Please visit sas.com/books to

- Sign up to review a book
- Request information on how to become a SAS Press author
- Recommend a topic
- Provide feedback on a book

Do you have questions about a SAS Press book that you are reading? Contact the author through saspress@sas.com.

Foreword

SAS® Viya™ is the latest enhancement to the SAS platform. It is designed to address the new, and increasingly diverse needs of organizations with new methods, access and options. SAS Viya addresses the complex analytical challenges of today, and effortlessly scales to meet your future needs, with cloud-enabled, elastic in-memory processing, in a high availability, multi-user environment.

SAS Viya complements SAS 9.4, enhancing the SAS platform to enable everyone – data scientists, business analysts, developers, and executives alike – to collaborate and achieve innovative results by unifying the entire analytics life cycle. Several groundbreaking papers have already been written to demonstrate how to use these techniques. We have carefully selected a handful of these from recent SAS Global Forum papers to introduce you to the topics and let you sample what each has to offer.

Mark Schneider - SAS® Viya™: What It Means for SAS® Administration

Not only does SAS Viya bring exciting advancements in high-performance analytics, it also takes a revolutionary step forward in the area of administration. The new SAS Cloud Analytics is accompanied by new management tools and techniques that are designed to ease the administrative burden while leveraging the open programming and visual interfaces that are standard among SAS Viya applications. This paper covers these concepts and then presents how you accomplish common deployment and administration tasks.

Jason Secosky - DATA Step in SAS® Viya™: Essential New Features

The DATA step is the familiar and powerful data processing language in SAS and now SAS Viya. The DATA step's simple syntax provides row-at-a-time operations to edit, restructure, and combine data. New to the DATA step in SAS Viya are a varying-length character data type and parallel execution. Varying-length character data enables intuitive string operations that go beyond the 32KB limit of current DATA step operations. This paper describes how the DATA step in SAS Viya can make your data processing simpler and faster.

Scott Mebust - The Future of Transpose: How SAS® Is Rebuilding Its Foundation by Making What Is Old New Again

As computer technology advances, SAS continually pursues opportunities to implement state-of-the-art systems that solve problems in data preparation and analysis faster and more efficiently. In this paper, we show how the TRANSPOSE procedure has been extended to operate in a distributed fashion within both Teradata and Hadoop, using dynamically generated DS2 executed by the SAS Embedded Process and within SAS Viya. With its new ability to work within these environments, PROC TRANSPOSE provides you with access to its parallel processing power and produces results that are compatible with your existing SAS programs.

Xiangxiang Meng and Kevin D Smith - <u>I Am Multilingual: A Comparison of the Python, Java, Lua, and REST Interfaces to SAS® Viya™</u>

The accessibility of SAS Viya emphasizes a unified experience for data scientists. You can now execute the analytic capabilities of SAS from different programming languages including Python, Java, and Lua, as well as use a RESTful endpoint to execute CAS actions directly. This paper provides an introduction to these programming language interfaces. For each language, we illustrate how the API is surfaced from the CAS server, the types of data that you can upload to a CAS server, and the result tables that are returned. This paper also provides a comprehensive comparison of using these programming languages to build a common analytical process, including connecting to a CAS server; exploring, manipulating, and visualizing data; and building statistical and machine learning models.

Jeff Diamond - <u>An Introduction to SAS® Visual Analytics 8.1</u>

This paper introduces SAS Visual Analytics 8.1. It is the tenth release of the software and the first release on SAS Viya. The interface has been completely rewritten in HTML5. It is a clean, modern interface with SAS Visual Analytics Designer and SAS Visual Analytics Explorer merged into a single application. The add-on SAS Visual Statistics is also fully integrated into this new web application. There is more. SAS Visual Data Mining and Machine Learning is also available as a fully integrated add-on. SAS Visual Analytics gives you a one-stop shop for all your interactive data exploration, modeling, and reporting.

Jonathan Wexler, Susan Haller, and Radhikha Myneni - <u>An Overview of SAS® Visual Data Mining and Machine Learning on SAS® Viya</u>

Machine learning is in high demand. Whether you are a citizen data scientist who wants to work interactively or you are a hands-on data scientist who wants to code, you have access to the latest analytic techniques with SAS Visual Data Mining and Machine Learning on SAS Viya. This paper describes in-memory machine-learning techniques such as gradient boosting, factorization machines, neural networks, and much more through its interactive visual interface, SAS Studio tasks, procedures, and a Python client.

Patrick Koch, Brett Wujek, Oleg Golovidov, and Steven Gardner - <u>Automated Hyperparameter Tuning for Effective Machine Learning</u>

Machine learning predictive modeling algorithms are governed by *hyperparameters* that have no clear defaults that work with a wide range of applications. The depth of a decision tree, the number of trees in a forest, the number of hidden layers and neurons in each layer in a neural network, and the degree of regularization to prevent overfitting are a few examples of quantities that must be prescribed for these algorithms. This paper presents an automatic tuning implementation that uses local search optimization for tuning hyperparameters of modeling algorithms in SAS Visual Data Mining and Machine Learning.

Funda Güneş, Russ Wolfinger, and Pei-Yi Tan - <u>Stacked Ensemble Models for Improved Prediction Accuracy</u>

Ensemble modeling is now a well-established means for improving prediction accuracy; it enables you to average out noise from diverse models and thereby enhance the generalizable signal. Basic stacked ensemble techniques combine predictions from multiple machine learning algorithms and use these predictions as inputs to second-level learning models. This paper shows how you can generate a diverse set of models by various methods such as forest, gradient boosted decision trees, factorization machines, and logistic regression and then combine them with stacked-ensemble techniques such as hill climbing, gradient boosting, and nonnegative least squares in SAS Visual Data Mining and Machine Learning.

Lawrie Elder - Counter Radicalization through Investigative Insights and Data Exploitation

Using SAS® Viya™

This end-to-end capability demonstration illustrates how SAS Viya can aid intelligence, homeland security, and law-enforcement agencies in counterterrorism activities. With SAS Viya, it is possible to integrate all aspects of the intelligence and investigation life cycles through standard, unified components that provide a foundation for sharing and communicating.

We hope these selections give you a useful overview of the power and adaptability of SAS Viya and its tools.

Randy Guard
Executive Vice President
Chief Marketing Officer

Randy Guard is responsible for the SAS brand, providing global, strategic direction and marketing vision for SAS products and solutions. He oversees several operational business units, including product management, global marketing, sales enablement, communications and creative services. Guard has many years of consulting, marketing and product development experience. He is responsible for the SAS portfolio, which spans analytics, data visualization, data management, business intelligence and industry solutions. Guard's extensive consulting background, along with a strong grasp of market dynamics, allows him to align marketing initiatives that position SAS at the forefront of new developments such as IoT, cybersecurity and cloud.

SAS® Viya™: What It Means for SAS® Administration

Mark Schneider, SAS Institute Inc.

ABSTRACT

Not only does SAS® Viya™ bring exciting advancements in high-performance analytics, it also takes a revolutionary step forward in the area of administration. SAS Viya's Cloud Analytic Services provides platform management tools and techniques that are designed to ease the administrative burden while leveraging the open programming and visual interfaces that are standard among SAS Viya applications.

Learn about the completely rewritten SAS® Environment Manager 3.2, which supports SAS Viya. It includes a cleaner HTML5-based user interface, more flexible and intuitive authorization windows, and user and group management that is integrated with your corporate Lightweight Directory Access Protocol (LDAP). Understand how authentication works in SAS Viya without metadata identities.

Discover the key differences between SAS® 9 and SAS Viya deployments, including installation and automated update-in-place strategies orchestrated by Ansible for hot fixes, maintenance, and new product versions alike. See how the new microservices and stateful servers are managed and monitored.

In general, gain a better understanding of the components of the SAS Viya architecture, and how they can be collectively managed to keep your environment available, secure, and performant for the users and processes you support.

INTRODUCTION

SAS Viya represents the next major evolution of the SAS platform, and the administration processes have evolved alongside. It's important to understand administration in the overall context of planning, deploying, and managing SAS software. Of course, you must also have a general grasp of the components of the architecture of SAS Viya. This paper will first cover these concepts, and then present the way in which you accomplish common deployment and administration tasks.

The information presented in this paper assumes a SAS Viya 3.2 deployment including both visual and programming interfaces. While it is possible to install SAS Viya solely with programming interfaces (in other words, SAS Studio, native Python, Java, Lua, and R language support, and REST API access), the drag-and-drop visual interface exemplified by web-based products like SAS Visual Analytics comes with several more servers and services to manage. SAS Viya provides a supporting utility to ease this burden.

SAS ADMINISTRATION LIFECYCLE

The process of planning, deploying, and administering SAS software falls under a common lifecycle depicted in Figure 1.

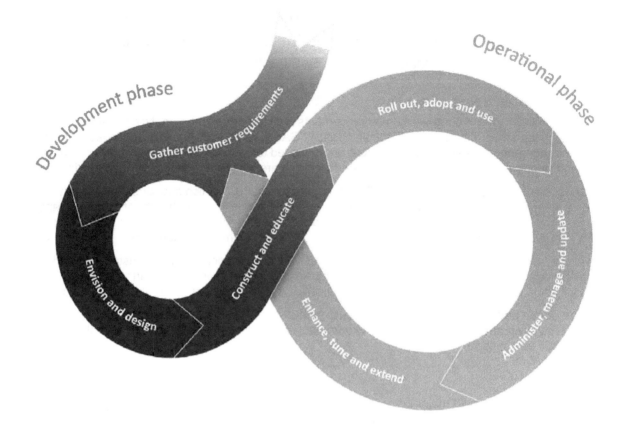

Figure 1. SAS Administration Lifecycle

This diagram represents a continuous process from requirement definition to environment administration and tuning, and back again to new requirement identification. Note that this lifecycle applies equally to SAS 9 and SAS Viya. For purposes of this paper, we will focus on the administrative aspects involved in the "Operational phase" portion of this diagram, and specifically in the context of SAS Viya.

ARCHITECTURE OF SAS VIYA

SAS Viya introduces several modern practices to the SAS Platform architecture. While SAS 9 brought a distributed client/server web-enabled model, with an extensible middle tier, several flavors of job execution servers, and a metadata server to govern them all, SAS Viya brings a more resilient, elastic, unified, and accessible architecture, which leverages cloud-friendly microservices and a next generation analytics run-time engine. Figure 2 shows a high-level architectural view of SAS Viya.

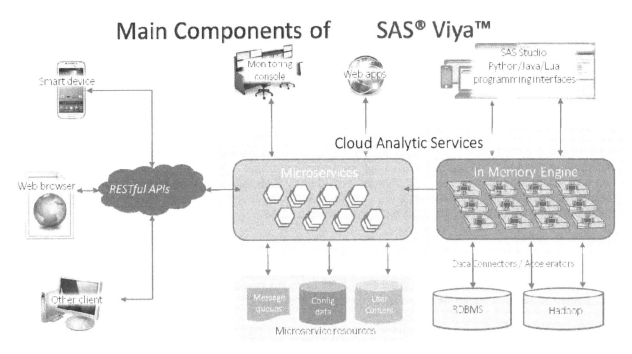

Figure 2. SAS Viya High-Level Architecture

To administer SAS Viya, you should have a good understanding of each of the following components.

SAS CLOUD ANALYTIC SERVICES

SAS Cloud Analytic Services (CAS) is the "heart and soul" of SAS Viya. It's where all the high-performance analytic processing occurs. It also contains a collection of microservices which effectively take on the responsibility of the middle tier along with other environment support functionality, like authentication and backup.

In-Memory Engine (CAS Server)

The CAS server is SAS Viya's run-time engine for analytics and data management. It is an in-memory server that can run on a single machine or be distributed across multiple machines. In a distributed deployment, it can dynamically scale up and down based on workload demands by adding or removing its underlying worker nodes.

Microservices

CAS microservices essentially break down the monolithic intelligence platform of SAS 9 into dozens of functional components, each doing exactly one thing and doing that one thing well. The value of microservices to an administrator is that they are independently scalable and updatable. Based on the function performed, you might need more instances of one microservice (for example, authorization) as opposed to another microservice (for example, backup). For a highly available deployment, you will want at least two instances of each microservice.

MONITORING CONSOLE

SAS Environment Manager is a centralized web application to monitor and administer SAS Viya. This includes SAS web applications, microservices, the CAS server, data connectors and data connect accelerators, and microservice resources. SAS Environment Manager is covered in detail in the Administration section of this paper.

WEB APPS

SAS Viya uses HTML5-based web applications to surface both administration and end-user functionality. A special web application, the SAS Environment Manager, provides a centralized monitoring console as well as general SAS administration support. We'll cover the details of its capability later in this paper. Licensed SAS solutions provide web applications like SAS Visual Analytics and Data Mining and Machine Learning, which leverage CAS to provide supporting analytic and data management actions.

PROGRAMMING INTERFACES

SAS Viya supports a variety of direct programming interfaces. As with SAS 9, SAS Studio is used to compose and submit jobs using the SAS programming language. Java, Python, and Lua programmers can take advantage of packages and libraries provided by SAS, which can be installed in these respective development environments (for example, within a Jupyter Notebook) to provide direct access to CAS actions without going through a client supplied by SAS.

RESTFUL APIS

CAS provides RESTful API support, which is essentially the integration language of the web, to enable web application developers to directly access CAS. Both the microservices and the CAS server are architected to surface public REST APIs for external consumption.

DATA CONNECTORS / ACCELERATORS

Like SAS 9, SAS Viya can access user data from a growing number of sources. SAS Data Connectors are the SAS Viya equivalent of SAS/ACCESS engines, and they allow serial access to a variety of data sources such as Teradata, Oracle, Postgres, and ODBC sources. SAS Data Connect Accelerators provide parallelized data access using the same SAS Embedded Process technology leveraged by SAS In-Database offerings provided in SAS 9. In fact, the same SAS Embedded Process software deployed to a database can simultaneously support parallel queries from SAS 9 and SAS Viya solutions.

MICROSERVICE RESOURCES

SAS microservices themselves are "stateless" in that they do not persist data. As such, they use microservice resources in the form of persistent data stores when they need to save user content (for example, folders, job definitions, and reports) and configuration data (for example, a list of services deployed and the options used to launch the services). They also report activity in the form of metrics and logs to message queues. SAS applications, user applications, and third-party administrative tools can subscribe to these queues in order to glean relevant real-time information about the SAS Viya operational environment.

DEPLOYMENT

One of the first things a SAS administrator will notice is that the SAS Viya deployment process is completely different from SAS 9. Industry-standard deployment tools are used rather than the SAS Deployment Wizard.

Figure 3 depicts how a SAS Viya deployment works.

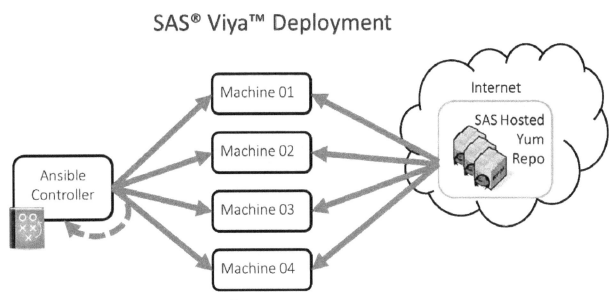

Figure 3. Ansible-based Deployment Process

ANSIBLE INSTALLATION

In a simple multi-machine deployment, the Linux standard Ansible orchestration tool is used to remotely install and configure software. Using an Ansible "playbook", which is emailed to you with your software order, you map different SAS Viya servers and services to specific machines in your network. Once mapped, Ansible uses SSH to execute installation commands on each of the target machines. These installation commands are Linux standard yum commands, which reach out to a yum repository hosted by SAS and download the associated software as Linux standard rpm packages, which can then be installed locally.

The Ansible controller machine from which you launch your deployment can serve as a target machine to receive SAS software, if you so choose. You can also set up a local "mirror" of the yum repository if your target machines do not have external Internet access.

The Ansible process checks certain system requirements, installs and configures the software, and starts all servers and services. Once this single command completes, you have an operational system. The first post-installation task is typically to hook up your corporate LDAP directory service to your SAS Viya deployment. You do this by using SAS Environment Manager, described in a later section of this paper.

One of the key advantages to the Ansible process is the way in which you download and install SAS software updates. In SAS 9, you downloaded and installed hot fixes and maintenance releases using SAS proprietary utilities such as the SAS Hot Fix Analysis, Download, and Deployment tool (SASHFADD), SAS Download Manager, SAS Deployment Wizard, and SAS Deployment Manager. All these utilities go away with SAS Viya. Instead, you simply rerun your Ansible playbook in order to download and install the rpm packages holding the latest versions of your SAS software components. If you maintain a yum repository mirror, you must first refresh your mirror prior to rerunning Ansible.

ENCRYPTION

Administrators are invariably concerned with securing their deployment, and encrypting traffic is a key component in any security strategy. Upon completing your install, you can configure your environment to encrypt data, which is transmitted among client and server processes (which is called "data in motion") as well as data persisted in CAS libraries and tables (which is called "data at rest").

You can encrypt data in motion for all of the following types of communication in a SAS Viya deployment:

- SAS Studio using HTTPS
- CAS Server Monitor using HTTPS
- Clients to the CAS server using transport layer security (TLS)
- Data Connect Accelerators to the CAS server using TLS
- SAS/CONNECT client to SAS/CONNECT spawner using TLS

The CAS server supports securing data at rest by providing encryption at both the data table level and the level of the containing CAS library. Consult the "Encryption" section of *SAS Viya 3.2 Administration* for details about enabling encryption for data in motion and data at rest.

ADMINISTRATION

SAS administrators will see dramatic changes in the way they go about managing their SAS Viya environments. While the types of activities performed – such as server management, securing resources, user management, and monitoring – haven't changed, the way in which you go about these tasks is quite a bit different from SAS 9.

One of the most significant changes is the absence of the SAS Metadata Server. Security information that was previously managed in the SAS Metadata Server is now in the new SAS Infrastructure Data Server, and configuration information is now in the new SAS Configuration Server. Both of these servers are managed using the SAS Environment Manager.

Details on these and other aspects of SAS Viya administration follow.

SAS ENVIRONMENT MANAGER

The SAS Environment Manager is the primary utility by which you perform various administrative functions. It is the "Monitoring console" in the architecture diagram shown in Figure 2. This web-based application was written from the ground up for SAS Viya, adopting the standard HTML5 interface used by other SAS Viya applications. Figure 4 shows the top-level dashboard for the SAS Environment Manager.

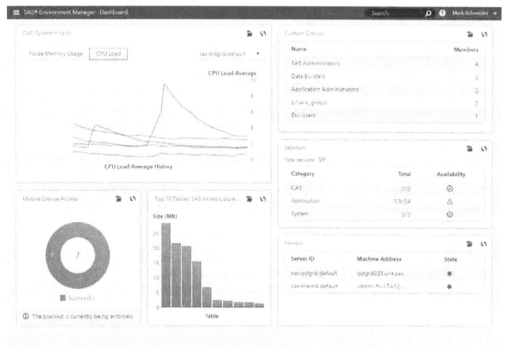

Figure 4. SAS Environment Manager Dashboard

The SAS Environment Manager provides control over the following functions.

Authentication

Authentication is about controlling who can log on to your environment. With SAS Viya, you connect to a preexisting corporate LDAP directory service or Security Assertion Markup Language (SAML) service provider in order to govern user logins. Unlike SAS 9, there is no repository specific to SAS of approved users. Using SAS Environment Manager, you can filter which LDAP user accounts are valid for SAS Viya.

See the "Configure Security" section of the *SAS Viya 3.2 Deployment Guide* for details about connecting to your directory service.

You can manage credentials used to connect to external data sources or Esri, and encryption keys applied to CAS data within the SAS Environment Manager under the **Security → Domains** menu.

Users and Groups

As mentioned, SAS Viya uses a corporate directory service to specify valid users. User information managed in LDAP is presented in read-only fashion in the SAS Environment Manager interface. This means you can manage your user information in one place – your existing directory service- but you can still see all your information within SAS Environment Manager.

LDAP groups are also conveyed as read-only entities within SAS Environment Manager. This means that you can take advantage of preexisting groups when establishing your SAS Viya security policy. In addition, you can create "custom" groups within SAS Viya that are not reflected in LDAP. SAS Viya is shipped with several predefined custom groups. The groups of particular interest to administrators are:

- SAS Administrators – These users can access all tasks in SAS Environment Manager, user content, and application functionality. This group is an "assumable" group, which means that when users belonging to this group log on, they are asked whether they want to "assume" the extra permissions associated with this group. Using assumable groups is a preventative measure to ensure that group members don't inadvertently execute unintended privileged tasks.

- Application Administrators – These users can manage application-specific administrative functions such as defining web themes and dictating the functions that appear for all users in the SAS Home top-level dashboard.

- Data Builders – These users have access to the SAS Visual Data Builder application.

- Esri Users – These users can access Esri systems for geographic map information.

Authorization

In SAS Viya, you can authorize users or groups to access data, user content, or application functionality. You can also authorize which mobile devices have access to the environment. Each of the arrows in the SAS Viya Architecture diagram in Figure 2 represents an access point subject to authorization.

To specify the authorization of a user or group for data, you use the SAS Environment Manager's Data menu to display the data being managed by the CAS server. If you select a particular library or table, you can choose to display the authorization settings related to the data. Figure 5 shows a typical Authorization window.

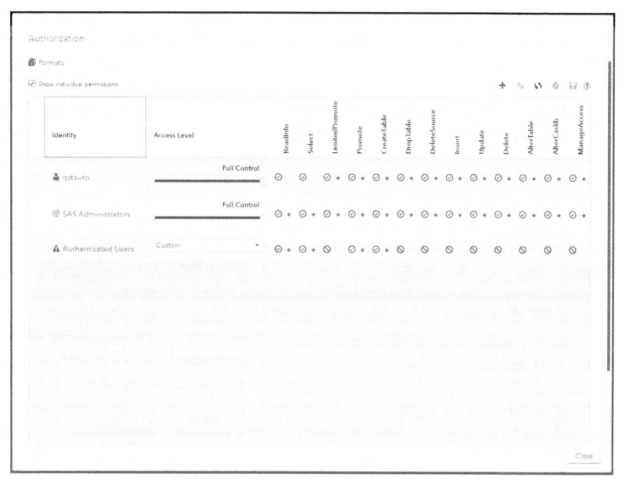

Figure 5. Authorization Window

Permissions can be assigned at a coarse level by using the Access Level slider (Full Control, Write, Read, No Access) or at a granular level (ReadInfo, Select, LimitedPromote, and so on). The granular level controls are specifically designed using terms a database administrator (DBA) is likely to understand.

A similar window is used when you set permissions on SAS Viya user content such as folders, reports, and jobs, although there are fewer permission values (Read, Update, Delete, Secure, Add, and Remove). Because user content is managed in a hierarchical folder structure, you can choose to have permissions conveyed to child members of a folder.

A more advanced type of authorization is surfaced in the form of rules. You can use the **Security →Rules** menu in SAS Environment Manager to control user access to functionality within SAS Viya (for example, controlling who has the ability to back up and restore your environment). You can also use rules to specify conditions on access to objects. For example, you can limit access to a particular report to certain times of the day.

Finally, you can authorize which mobile devices can connect to SAS Viya via the **Security → Mobile Devices** menu in SAS Environment Manager. You can either set up a blacklist of disallowed devices, or a whitelist of permitted devices.

8

Configuration

Most SAS Viya configuration occurs automatically when you deploy your software. However, there are times when an administrator needs to adjust certain parameters related to the services running in their environment (which are the "Microservices", the "In-Memory Engine", and the "Microservice resources" in Figure 2). Examples include:

- LDAP settings – See description in the Authentication section
- Memory allocation
- Time-out values

Logging levels – See description in the Data

At the heart of any SAS Viya deployment is the data that is maintained in the CAS server (the "In-Memory Engine" in Figure 2). CAS tables are distributed across the memory space of a CAS server's worker nodes, allowing for high-performance distributed processing. The CAS server also allocates "spillover" disk space, which is used for unused blocks of CAS tables in order to provide a larger virtual memory footprint. This spillover space is invisible to the file system outside of CAS, so no other processes can gain access to these data blocks. Administrators can disable the spillover feature, but it is on by default because the underlying algorithm is optimized to not hamper performance.

CAS tables are organized into CAS-specific libraries, or "caslibs." A caslib defines both a source location from whence data is loaded (such as a directory path accessible to the CAS server or a Hadoop location) and a location within the CAS server where the data is accessed once loaded. Caslibs can either be isolated to a particular user's running session (session scope) or shared with other users of the CAS server (global scope).

The SAS Environment Manager **Data** menu allows an administrator to view all global scope caslibs and their contained tables. Figure 6 shows a listing of all the tables within a caslib. The **State** column indicates whether a table is loaded into memory within the CAS server.

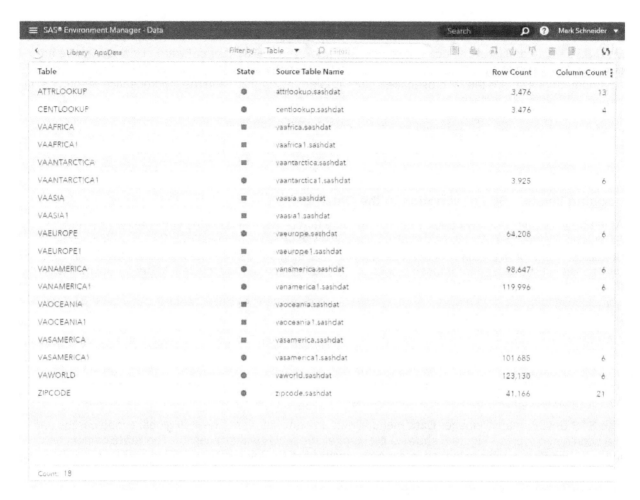

Figure 6. Data Tables in a Caslib

You can set permissions on tables in a caslib by using the Authorization window, which is available from this listing and shown in Figure 5. Although members of the SAS Administrators custom group have access to all content and functionality within SAS Environment Manager, they do not necessarily have access to all CAS data. Such universal data access is granted to a CAS server "Superuser." By default, the SAS Administrators custom group is added to the list of users who are able to assume the Superuser role. As a precaution, SAS Environment Manager users who opt in to the SAS Administrators assumable group at login (see a description of assumable groups in the Users and Groups section of this paper) do not by default assume the Superuser role. They must do so explicitly by going to the associated CAS server in the list of servers under the **Data** menu, and choosing to "Assume the Superuser role."

User Content

Users of SAS Viya applications like SAS Visual Analytics can save their content in a folder structure. This content is maintained in the "User Content database" shown under Microservice resources in Figure 2. When a user first logs in, the system automatically creates a personal folder for the user. They can then create their own folder structure underneath this folder and store reports, plans, and other content within the structure. They can define this folder structure either in SAS Environment Manager or in client applications such as SAS Visual Analytics.

As an administrator, you can view the entire folder structure and its contents under the **Content** menu of SAS Environment Manager. From here, you can set permissions on individual objects or their containing folders in order to share them with others.

- Logging section

- Esri map service location

You adjust service configuration settings under the **Resources → Configuration** menu of SAS Environment Manager. The configuration settings for a particular service are stored in a collection of "configuration instances." Each configuration instance is created from a parent "configuration definition," and comprises a collection of name-value pairs used by the service. This approach allows many services to share configuration instances from the same configuration definition.

Data

At the heart of any SAS Viya deployment is the data that is maintained in the CAS server (the "In-Memory Engine" in Figure 2). CAS tables are distributed across the memory space of a CAS server's worker nodes, allowing for high-performance distributed processing. The CAS server also allocates "spillover" disk space, which is used for unused blocks of CAS tables in order to provide a larger virtual memory footprint. This spillover space is invisible to the file system outside of CAS, so no other processes can gain access to these data blocks. Administrators can disable the spillover feature, but it is on by default because the underlying algorithm is optimized to not hamper performance.

CAS tables are organized into CAS-specific libraries, or "caslibs." A caslib defines both a source location from whence data is loaded (such as a directory path accessible to the CAS server or a Hadoop location) and a location within the CAS server where the data is accessed once loaded. Caslibs can either be isolated to a particular user's running session (session scope) or shared with other users of the CAS server (global scope).

The SAS Environment Manager **Data** menu allows an administrator to view all global scope caslibs and their contained tables. Figure 6 shows a listing of all the tables within a caslib. The **State** column indicates whether a table is loaded into memory within the CAS server.

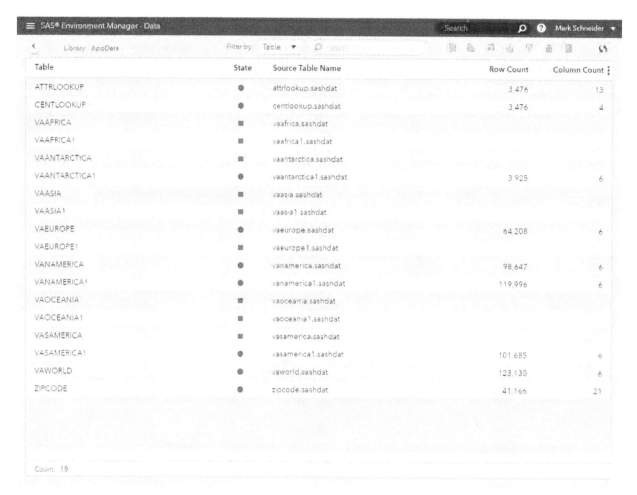

Figure 6. Data Tables in a Caslib

You can set permissions on tables in a caslib by using the Authorization window, which is available from this listing and shown in Figure 5. Although members of the SAS Administrators custom group have access to all content and functionality within SAS Environment Manager, they do not necessarily have access to all CAS data. Such universal data access is granted to a CAS server "Superuser." By default, the SAS Administrators custom group is added to the list of users who are able to assume the Superuser role. As a precaution, SAS Environment Manager users who opt in to the SAS Administrators assumable group at login (see a description of assumable groups in the Users and Groups section of this paper) do not by default assume the Superuser role. They must do so explicitly by going to the associated CAS server in the list of servers under the **Data** menu, and choosing to "Assume the Superuser role."

User Content

Users of SAS Viya applications like SAS Visual Analytics can save their content in a folder structure. This content is maintained in the "User Content database" shown under Microservice resources in Figure 2. When a user first logs in, the system automatically creates a personal folder for the user. They can then create their own folder structure underneath this folder and store reports, plans, and other content within the structure. They can define this folder structure either in SAS Environment Manager or in client applications such as SAS Visual Analytics.

As an administrator, you can view the entire folder structure and its contents under the **Content** menu of SAS Environment Manager. From here, you can set permissions on individual objects or their containing folders in order to share them with others.

Logging

All of the servers and services in a SAS Viya environment produce log files, which are stored in the following location:

```
/opt/sas/<deployment_name>/config/var/log/<productName>
```

where <deployment_name> is a unique identifier (typically something like "viya") assigned at deployment time in order to differentiate one SAS Viya deployment from another on the same machine. For convenience, the deployment process creates a symlink from `/var/log/sas/viya` to the above directory structure so that you can access your SAS Viya logs alongside other software logs on your system.

Logging threshold levels for services are set using the **Resources → Configuration** menu of SAS Environment Manager. Figure 7 shows the window used to view and set the logging level for a service, in this case the one used for rendering reports. From here, you can dynamically adjust the amount of detail a particular service writes to its log. For example, you might want to increase the logging level to DEBUG while diagnosing a problem with a service. There is no need to restart a service in order to pick up this change.

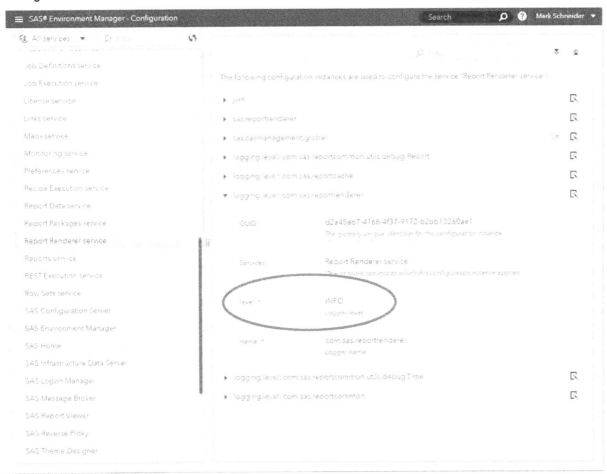

Figure 7. Logging Level for Report Renderer Service

SAS Viya environments include a collection of servers whose logging levels and content are controlled in the same way as they were in SAS 9 – with corresponding logconfig.xml files, which specify "loggers" and "appenders." These servers include the CAS server, the SAS workspace server, and the SAS/CONNECT server.

Monitoring

As shown earlier (Figure 4), the SAS Environment Manager dashboard provides a top-level view of several health indicators related to your environment. From it, you can view the following indicators:

- Memory and CPU usage for all CAS server nodes
- Mobile devices that have accessed or attempted to access your environment
- The SAS Infrastructure Data Server database size
- The most heavily-populated custom groups
- Service availability
- Server status

The dashboard provides a snapshot of the latest information, and is refreshed dynamically.

Many other health and performance metrics are available for viewing, and can be found under the **Resources → Machines and Services** windows. You can view metrics associated with a machine in your environment, or drill down to a specific service instance running on a machine and view its metrics. You can also view individual CAS sessions by drilling to their parent CAS service instance.

Additional monitoring capabilities are available via the CAS Server Monitor and Grid Monitor utilities, which are described in the "Monitoring" section of *SAS Viya 3.2 Administration*.

COMMAND-LINE INTERFACE

While you can accomplish many administrative tasks through the SAS Environment Manager interface, some tasks are currently only available by executing commands from an operating system console or in a batch script. SAS Viya provides a standard CLI (command-line interface) as well as REST API support for many of its features, including administrative tasks. You can find a full description of the standard CLI syntax in the "Using the Command-Line Interface" section of *SAS Viya 3.2 Administration*.

Two specific areas of administration that are currently isolated to command-line access are backing up your environment, and promoting content from one environment to another. Backups use REST APIs, while content promotion uses the standard SAS Viya CLI syntax. These are described below.

Backup and Restore

Prior to executing SAS Viya environment backups, you must specify your backup vault location within the **Resources → Configuration** window in SAS Environment Manager. There are other configuration settings you can adjust here, including a backup job time-out value and the retention period for backups stored in your vault.

Because you use REST API calls to execute SAS Viya backups and restores, it is convenient to use the Linux "curl" command as a wrapper for the calls. The following command is a template for such a call:

```
curl -X POST <Header including identity information> \
     <Execution Options> \
     <URI for the backup API>
```

You would substitute values for fields in angle brackets (<>). "URI" is the Uniform Resource Identifier, which uniquely identifies the backup RESTful interface resource.

When you run a backup, the associated files are first stored locally on the machines where the data resides. The backup files are then automatically transferred to the aforementioned central backup vault. If any portion of the backup fails, whether it be because of an unresponsive data source, an inability to store backup files locally, or a problem with transferring the files to the vault, the entire backup is considered to have failed and must be rerun.

For more details about SAS Viya backup and restore functionality, please consult the "Backup and Recovery" section of *SAS Viya 3.2 Administration*.

Content Promotion

You can transfer content from one SAS deployment to another. You can also transfer select content (for example, SAS Visual Analytics reports) across SAS 9.4 deployment to a SAS Viya deployment. Both tasks leverage the sas-transfer command-line interface. You download this interface to a client machine by accessing its URL in a browser. For example, on Linux, the URL would be:

```
<SAS_Viya_URL>/transfer/cli/linux/sas-transfer
```

You first need to determine the Uniform Resource Identifier (URI) of the content you want to promote using the sas-transfer command. You can easily discover the URI by navigating to the containing folder under the **Content** menu of SAS Environment Manager and selecting the item you want to transfer. Figure 8 shows the selection of a report in the Public folder (the one in which all authenticated SAS Viya users are allowed to store content by default).

Figure 8. URI of Report in Public Folder

After you determine the URI, you can execute commands to authenticate to your source SAS Viya environment and create a promotion package. You then authenticate to your target SAS Viya environment and import the package. An example of a typical SAS Viya command that creates a promotion package follows:

```
sas-transfer --profile SourceViya export \
        --resourceUri "<URI_from_SAS_Environment_Manager>" \
        --name "My Promotion Package"
```

See the "Promotion (Import and Export)" section of *SAS Viya 3.2 Administration* for more details about content promotion.

CONCLUSION

With its diverse, scalable, and powerful capabilities, SAS Viya brings a lot of additional value to your organization and your existing SAS deployment. With that value come new techniques to plan, deploy, and administer your environment. In many cases, those techniques are simplified when compared to SAS 9. These include deployments orchestrated by Ansible, LDAP integration for user management, and dynamic updates of system settings like logging levels. Investing time in learning the new architecture, and the tools that manage it, will pay off in time savings and increased uptime – two things that are always at a premium for SAS administrators.

RESOURCES

- SAS Institute Inc. 2017. *SAS Viya 3.2 Administration*. Cary NC: SAS Institute Inc. Available at http://support.sas.com/documentation/productaz/index.html#v

- SAS Institute Inc. 2017. *SAS Viya 3.2 Deployment Guide*. Cary NC: SAS Institute Inc. Available at http://support.sas.com/documentation/productaz/index.html#v

CONTACT INFORMATION

Your comments and questions are valued and encouraged. Contact the author at:

Mark Schneider
100 SAS Campus Drive
Cary NC 27513
SAS Institute Inc.
mark.schneider@sas.com
http://www.sas.com

An Overview of SAS® Visual Data Mining and Machine Learning on SAS® Viya

Jonathan Wexler, Susan Haller, and Radhikha Myneni, SAS Institute Inc., Cary, NC

ABSTRACT

Machine learning is in high demand. Whether you are a citizen data scientist who wants to work interactively or you are a hands-on data scientist who wants to code, you have access to the latest analytic techniques with SAS® Visual Data Mining and Machine Learning on SAS® Viya. This offering surfaces in-memory machine-learning techniques such as gradient boosting, factorization machines, neural networks, and much more through its interactive visual interface, SAS® Studio tasks, procedures, and a Python client. Learn about this multi-faceted new product and see it in action.

INTRODUCTION

Solving modern business problems often requires analytics that encompass multiple algorithmic disciplines, data that is both structured and unstructured, multiple programming languages, and – most importantly – collaboration within and across teams of varying skill sets. Addressing and solving business problems should not be constrained by technology. Technology enables analysts to solve problems from multiple angles. Likewise, computing power is cheap. Problems that were once deemed unsolvable using neural networks can now be run in mere seconds.

This paper shows you how to solve business problems, quickly and collaboratively, using SAS Visual Data Mining and Machine Learning on SAS Viya. This new offering enables you to interactively explore your data to uncover 'signal' in your data. Next you can programmatically analyze your data using a rich set of SAS procedures covering Statistics, Machine Learning, and Text Mining. You can add new input features using in-memory SAS DATA step. Utilize new tasks in SAS Studio on the SAS Viya platform to automatically generate the SAS code. If you prefer to write Python, access SAS Viya methods with the Python API. No matter the interface or language, SAS Viya enables you to start your analysis and continue forward without any roadblocks.

In this paper, you will learn how to access these methods through a case study.

SAS VISUAL DATA MINING AND MACHINE LEARNING ON SAS VIYA

SAS Viya is the foundation upon which the analytical toolset in this paper is installed. The components are modular by design. At its core, SAS Viya is built upon a common analytic framework, using 'actions'. These actions are atomic analytic activities, such as selecting variables, building models, generating results, and outputting score code. As shown in Figure 1, these actions can be accessed via SAS procedures, SAS applications, RESTful services, Java, Lua, and Python.

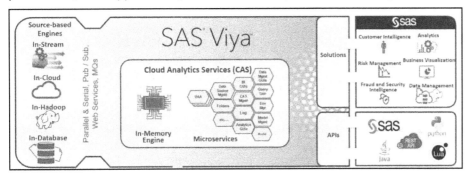

Figure 1. SAS Viya Ecosystem Is Open and Modular

SUPPORTED SAS VIYA ALGORITHMS

From a data mining and machine learning perspective, SAS Visual Data Mining and Machine Learning on SAS Viya enables end-to-end analytics - data wrangling, model building, and model assessment.

As shown in Table 1, the following methods are available to users:

Data Wrangling	Modeling
Binning	Logistic Regression
Cardinality	Linear Regression
Imputation	Generalized Linear Models
Transformations	Nonlinear Regression
Transpose	Ordinary Least Squares Regression
SQL	Partial Least Squares Regression
Sampling	Quantile Regression
Variable Selection	Decision Trees
Principal Components Analysis (PCA)	Forest
K-Means Clustering	Gradient Boosting
Moving Window PCA	Neural Network
Robust PCA	Support Vector Machines
	Factorization Machines
	Network / Community Detection
	Text Mining
	Support Vector Data Description

Table 1. Analytic Methods Available in SAS Visual Data Mining and Machine Learning on SAS Viya

You will experience increased productivity when using the aforementioned methods. All of these methods run in-memory, and take advantage of the parallel processing ability of your underlying infrastructure. The more nodes you have; the higher degree of parallelism you will experience when running. Once data is loaded to memory up-front, you can run sequential procedures against the same table in memory, eliminating the need to drop the data to disk after each run. You can continue your analysis using the same data in-memory. If the memory of your problem requires more memory than is available, the processing will continue over to disk.

There were numerous analytic innovations that we introduced with SAS Viya. At the head of the class is hyperparameter autotuning (Koch, Wujek, Golovidov, and Gardner 2017). When data scientists tune models, they train the models to determine the best model parameters to relate the input to a target. When they tune a model, they determine the architecture or best algorithmic hyperparameters that maximize predictability on an independent data set. Autotuning eliminates the need for random grid search or in a SAS user's case, running repetitive procedure calls with different properties. As shown in Figure 2, Autotuning uses a local search optimization methodology to intelligently search the hyperparameter space for the best combination of values that addresses the model objective – that is, misclassification, Lift, KS, and so on. Autotuning is available for Decision Trees, Neural Networks, Support Vector Machines, Forests, Gradient Boosting, and Factorization Machines.

Also new in SAS Viya are enhanced feature engineering techniques like Robust PCA (RPCA), Moving Window PCA, and the capability to detect outliers using Support Vector Data Description (SVDD). Robust PCA decomposes an input matrix into low-rank and sparse matrices. The low-rank matrix is more stable as the distortions in the data are moved into the sparse matrix, hence the term robust. Moving Window PCA captures the changes in principal components over time using sliding windows and you can choose RPCA to be performed in each window. SVDD is a machine learning technique where the model builds a minimum radius sphere around the training data and scores new observations by comparing the observation's distance from sphere center with the sphere radius. Thus, an observation outside the sphere is classified as an outlier.

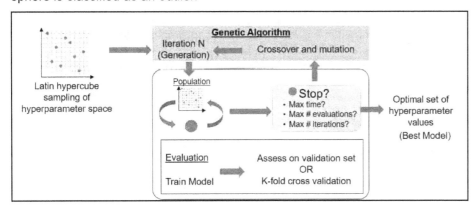

Figure 2. Autotuning Uses Optimization to Find the Best Set of Hyperparameters to Minimize Error

SAS VISUAL DATA MINING AND MACHINE LEARNING PRIMARY ANALYTIC INTERFACES

There are three primary interfaces we will cover in this paper. From within each tool, you can extend your analysis into one of the others. Data can be shared, and models can be extended and compared.

VISUAL ANALYTICS

SAS Visual Analytics enables drag-and-drop, exploratory visualization and modeling. Data must be loaded into memory, otherwise known as SAS Cloud Analytic Services (CAS). Once in CAS, you can interactively explore your data using visuals such as scatter plots, waterfall charts, bubble plots, time series plots and many more. As shown in Figure 3, you can further analyze your data using a set of statistics techniques including Clustering, Decision Trees, Generalized Linear Models, Linear Regression, and Logistic Regression. You can expand upon these models using the latest machine learning techniques including Factorization Machines, Forests, Gradient Boosting, Neural Networks, and Support Vector Machines.

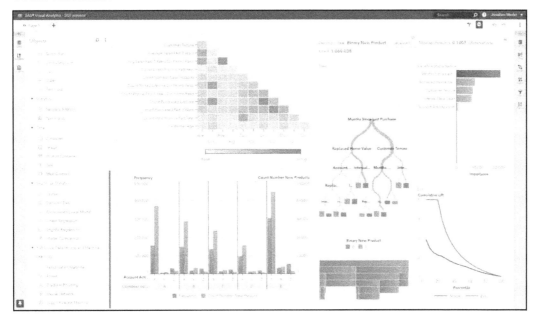

Figure 3. Interactive Visualization, Exploration, and Modeling Using SAS Visual Analytics

SAS STUDIO

SAS® Studio enables browser-based, programmatic access to the methods in SAS Viya. Using a modern, easy-to-use interface, you can run the exact same methods, and get the exact same answers as you would have with SAS Visual Analytics. As shown in Figure 4, you can programmatically run the methods from SAS Viya using in-memory procedures and SAS DATA step. Yes, the SAS DATA step now runs in-memory! There are several SAS Studio tasks that serve as code generators, so you have a way to learn and run these methods.

Figure 4. Access the SAS Viya Methods Using the SAS Language within SAS Studio

JUPYTER NOTEBOOK / PYTHON API

You can access the SAS Viya methods using the Python API to SAS Viya. The same methods that you can access in SAS Visual Analytics and SAS Studio are exposed from Python. A shown in Figure 5, you can access SAS Viya using a Jupyter notebook. Using a familiar Python construct, you can programmatically analyze your data, without any prior SAS knowledge.

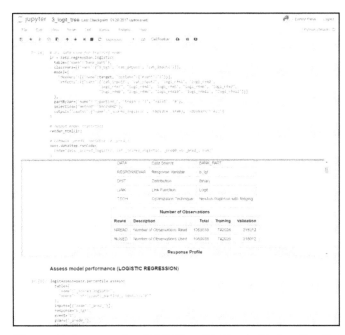

Figure 5. Access the SAS Viya Methods Using the Python API to SAS Viya

CASE STUDY

The BANK data set contains more than one million observations (rows) and 24 variables (columns) for this case study. The data set comes from a large financial services firm and represents consumers' home equity lines of credit, their automobile loans, and other types of short to medium-term credit instruments. Note that the data has been anonymized and transformed to conform to the regulation guidelines.

Though three target variables are available in the data set, the primary focus is on the binary target variable B_TGT, which indicates consumer accounts that bought at least one product in the previous campaign season. A campaign season at the bank runs for half a year and encompasses all marketing efforts to motivate the purchase (contracting) of the bank's financial services products. Campaign promotions are categorized into direct and indirect -- direct promotions consist of sales offers to a particular account that involve an incentive while indirect promotions are marketing efforts that do not involve an incentive.

In addition to the account identifier (**Account ID**), the following tables describe the variables in the data set:

Name	Label	Description
B_TGT	Tgt Binary New Product	A binary target variable. Accounts coded with a 1 contracted for at least one product in the previous campaign season. Accounts coded with a 0 did not contract for a product in the previous campaign season.
INT_TGT	Tgt Interval New Sales	The amount of financial services product (sum of sales) per account in the previous campaign season, denominated in US dollars.
CNT_TGT	Tgt Count Number New Products	The number of financial services products (count) per account in the previous campaign season.

Table 2. Target Variables Quantify Account Responses over the Current Campaign Season.

5

Name	Label	Description
CAT_INPUT1	Category 1 Account Activity Level	A three-level categorical variable that codes the activity of each account. • X → high activity. The account enters the current campaign period with a lot of products. • Y → average activity. • Z → low activity.
CAT_INPUT2	Category 2 Customer Value Level	A five-level (A-E) categorical variable that codes customer value. For example, the most profitable and creditworthy customers are coded with an A.

Table 3. Categorical Inputs Summarize Account-level Attributes Related to the Propensity to Buy Products and Other Characteristics Related to Profitability and Creditworthiness. These Variables Have Been Transformed to Anonymize Account-level Information and to Mitigate Quality Issues Related to Excessive Cardinality.

Name	Label	Description
RFM1	RFM1 Average Sales Past 3 Years	Average sales amount attributed to each account over the past three years
RFM2	RFM2 Average Sales Lifetime	Average sales amount attributed to each account over the account's tenure
RFM3	RFM3 Avg Sales Past 3 Years Dir Promo Resp	Average sales amount attributed to each account in the past three years in response to a direct promotion
RFM4	RFM4 Last Product Purchase Amount	Amount of the last product purchased
RFM5	RFM5 Count Purchased Past 3 Years	Number of products purchased in the past three years
RFM6	RFM6 Count Purchased Lifetime	Total number of products purchased in each account's tenure.
RFM7	RFM7 Count Prchsd Past 3 Years Dir Promo Resp	Number of products purchased in the previous three years in response to a direct promotion
RFM8	RFM8 Count Prchsd Lifetime Dir Promo Resp	Total number of products purchased in the account's tenure in response to a direct promotion
RFM9	RFM9 Months Since Last Purchase	Months since the last product purchase
RFM10	RFM10 Count Total Promos Past Year	Number of total promotions received by each account in the past year
RFM11	RFM11 Count Direct Promos Past Year	Number of direct promotions received by each account in the past year
RFM12	RFM12 Customer Tenure	Customer tenure in months.

Table 4. Interval Inputs Provide Continuous Measures on Account-level Attributes Related to the

Recency, Frequency, and Sales Amounts (RFM). All Measures below Correspond to Activity Prior to the Current Campaign Season.

Name	Label	Description
DEMOG_AGE	Demog Customer Age	Average age in each account's demographic region
DEMOG_GENF	Demog Female Binary	A categorical variable that is 1 if the primary holder of the account if female and 0 otherwise.
DEMOG_GENM	Demog Male Binary	A categorical variable that is 1 if the primary holder of the account is male and 0 otherwise
DEMOG_HO	Demog Homeowner Binary	A categorical variable that is 1 if the primary holder of the account is a homeowner and 0 otherwise.
DEMOG_HOMEVAL	Demog Home Value	Average home value in each account's demographic region
DEMOG_INC	Demog Income	Average income in each account's demographic region
DEMOG_PR	Demog Percentage Retired	The percentage of retired people in each account's demographic region

Table 5. Demographic Variables Describe the Profile of Each Account in Terms of Income, Homeownership, and Other Characteristics.

LOAD LOCAL DATA TO IN-MEMORY LIBRARY

Before we start our analysis, we will use SAS Studio to load the local data to memory, so that it is accessible by our analytics team both visually and programmatically. We will then create a validation holdout set in order to assess our models.

The first LIBNAME statement automatically starts a CAS session, attached to the public caslib. Caslibs are in-memory locations that contain tables, access controls, and information about data sources. We are using the public caslib since this location is accessible by our team. In SAS Studio mycaslib is a library reference to the public caslib and will be referred to by SAS Viya procedures and any SAS DATA steps. The second LIBNAME statement is linked to the local file system that contains our SAS data set.

```
libname mycaslib cas caslib=public;
libname locallib 'your_local_library';
```

We will use PROC CASUTIL to load our local data to the public caslib. Using the 'promote' option enables us to make the data available to all CAS sessions. By default, tables in CAS sessions have local scope, so promoting enables you to access the in-memory table across multiple sessions and users.

```
proc casutil;
   load data=locallib.bank OUTCASLIB="public" casout="bank" promote;
run;
```

We will run PROC PARTITION to randomly separate our data into training and validation partitions. A new variable _partind_ will be assigned two numeric values: 1 for training data and 2 for validation data. The seed option allows you to re-create the random sample in future CAS sessions on the same CAS server. This is valuable when trying to reproduce results with multiple users. You should include the copyvars option if you want to keep all source variables in your partitioned data set.

```
proc partition data=mycaslib.bank partition samppct=70 seed=12345;
  by b_tgt;
  output out=mycaslib.bank_part copyvars=(_ALL_);
run;
```

BUILD MODELS INTERACTIVELY USING VISUAL ANALYTICS

Once the data is loaded and promoted to the public caslib, it is accessible from within SAS Visual Analytics. The first model we will create is a Gradient Boosting model, which trains a series of decision trees successively to fit the residual of the prediction from the earlier trees in the series. The target in this model is b_tgt. We will set the number of trees to 50. There are other regularization options such as Lasso and Ridge that can help prevent overfitting. As you change options, the visualization is recomputed in near real time, taking just a few seconds.

Note that misclassification for the validation partition is 0.1598. The first visualization, on the left, is the Variable Importance plot. This plot displays each variable's importance in the model. See that rfm5, rfm9, and demog_homeval are proportionately more important than the other predictors. The next plot is the Iteration plot, which indicates how well the model classified as the number of trees increased. In this case, the misclassification rate tails off after about 30 trees. The bottom right plot indicates how well the model assessed in terms of lift, misclassification, and ROC.

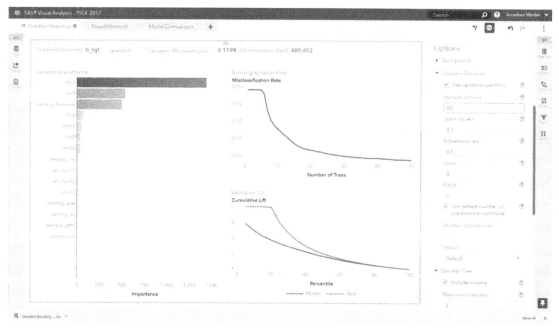

Figure 6. Interactive Gradient Boosting in SAS Visual Analytics

The next model we will build is a Neural Network, which is a statistical model that is designed to mimic the biological structures of the human brain that contains an input layer, multiple hidden layers, an output layer, and the connections between each of those.

Note that misclassification for the validation partition is 0.1970. The Network plot illustrates the relationship between your inputs and hidden layers. The next plot is the Iteration plot, which reports on the Objective/Loss function as the number of iterations increased. It appears that the Objective/Loss flattens around 20 iterations. You can tune the model further by changing the number of hidden layers, the number of neurons in each hidden layer, activation function for each layer, or other options.

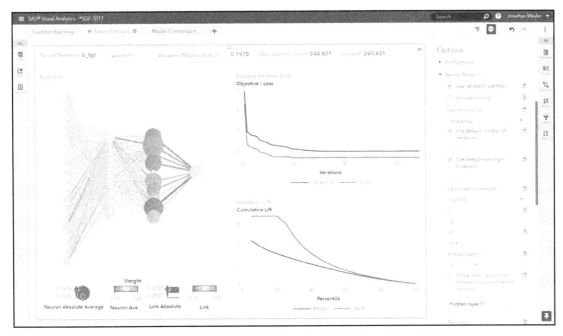

Figure 7. Interactive Two-Layer Neural Network in SAS Visual Analytics

The Model Comparison automatically chooses the best model based on the fit statistic selected in the Options panel. In this case, the model with the lowest misclassification rate is chosen. Note the partition, response, and event level much match across each model in order to generate the report. Gradient Boosting is selected as the champion model.

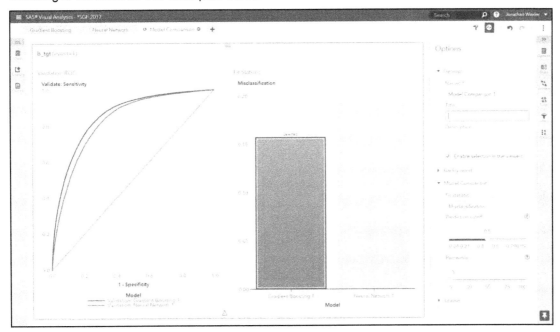

Figure 8. Interactive Model Comparison in SAS Visual Analytics

We will export the Gradient Boosting model so that it is accessible from SAS Studio in the next section. This model information will automatically be stored in the 'models' caslib as a binary analytic store (or astore) file.

Figure 9. Exporting Gradient Boosting Score Code from SAS Visual Analytics

BUILD MODELS PROGRAMATICALLY USING SAS STUDIO

Now that we have explored our data and built interactive models within SAS Visual Analytics to predict b_tgt, we might want to extend our analysis and build additional models within SAS Studio, our programmatic environment. Prior to building our models within SAS Visual Analytics, we created and promoted the BANK_PART CAS table to the public caslib so that it is available across multiple sessions and multiple users. In addition, this table contains a _partind_ variable to represent our training and validation partitions. The LIBNAME statement below points to this public caslib and allows the user within SAS Studio to build models with the same table that was loaded into memory and used to build our interactive models in SAS Visual Analytics.

```
libname mycaslib cas caslib=public;
```

The first step in our modeling process is to further "wrangle" our data. In this case, we have identified several predictors that have a high percentage of missing values. In order to address this, we will first run PROC VARIMPUTE to replace these missing values with the calculated mean of all of the nonmissing observations.

```
%let partitioned_data - mycaslib.bank_part;

proc varimpute data=&partitioned_data.;
  input demog_age demog_homeval demog_inc rfm3  /ctech=mean;
  output out=mycaslib.bank_prepped_temp copyvars=(_ALL_);
  code file="&outdir./impute_score.sas";
run;
```

Next, we might want to apply transformations to a few of the continuous predictors. These transformations can be done using in-memory SAS DATA step code. Notice that the data being used to build these transformations as well as the output table that is being created are both pointing to a caslib. When this is the case, the SAS DATA step code is run automatically in-memory without requiring any special requests. This table is then promoted with the PROMOTE=YES option so that it can be used later if we want to continue the model building process with these new variables in an environment such as Python. We will show this type of integration in the next section.

```
%let prepped_data = mycaslib.bank_prepped;
data &prepped_data (promote=YES);
  set mycaslib.bank_prepped_temp ;

  if (IM_RFM3 > 0) then LOG_IM_RFM3 = LOG(IM_RFM3);
  else LOG_IM_RFM3 = .;

  if (RFM1 > 0) then LOG_RFM1 = LOG(RFM1);
  else LOG_RFM1 = .;
run;
```

The first model we will build is a Decision Tree model. Decision Trees use a sequence of simple if-then-else rules to make a prediction or to classify an output. We will build this model with PROC TREESPLIT using the Entropy growing criterion and then apply the C45 methodology to select the optimal tree, which is based on the validation partition. We store the details of this tree model in the score code file treeselect_score.sas. This score code is applied to the bank data creating new columns that contain the predicted value for each observation.

```
/* Specify the data set inputs and target */
%let class_inputs    = cat_input1 cat_input2 demog_ho demog_genf
                       demog_genm;
%let interval_inputs = IM_demog_age IM_demog_homeval IM_demog_inc
                       demog_pr log_rfm1 rfm2 log_im_rfm3 rfm4-rfm12 ;
%let target          = b_tgt;

/* DECISION TREE predictive model                                  */
proc treesplit data=&prepped_data.;
  input &interval_inputs. / level=interval;
  input &class_inputs. / level=nominal;
  target &target. / level=nominal;
  partition rolevar=_partind_ (train='1' validate='0');
  grow entropy;
  prune c45;
  code file="&outdir./treeselect_score.sas";
run;

/* Score the data using the generated tree model score code        */
data mycaslib._scored_tree;
  set &prepped_data.;
  %include "&outdir./treeselect_score.sas";
run;
```

In Figure 10, we see a partial tree diagram that was created from running PROC TREESPLIT. This shows that the first rule applied to the data was based on the predictor rfm5. Those observations that have a value for rfm5 that was less than or equal to 3.6 were passed into the left hand branch; those with a value of rfm5 that was greater than 3.6 were passed into the right hand branch. You can continue to follow the rules down the entire branch of a tree until arriving at the final node, which determines your classification.

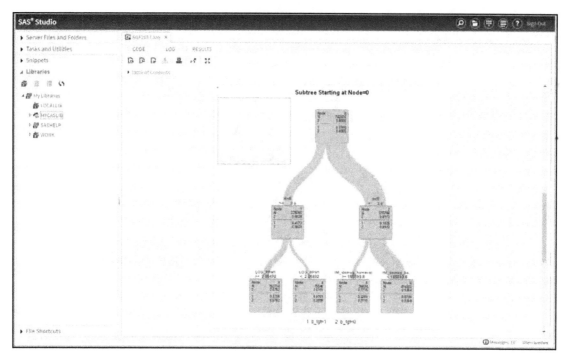

Figure 10. Decision Tree Subtree Diagram from SAS Studio

Note that the misclassification for the validation partition is 0.1447. The Variable Importance table reports the relative importance of all of the predictors that were used in building this model. We can see from this table that rfm5, LOG_RFM1, IM_demog_homeval, and rfm9 were the predictors that contributed the most in defining the splitting rules that made up this particular decision tree model.

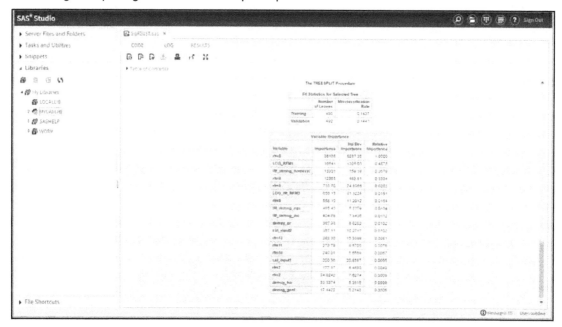

Figure 11. Decision Tree Fit Statistics and Variable Importance Metrics from SAS Studio

The next model that we will build is a Forest model. A Forest is an ensemble of individual trees where the final classification is based on an average of the probabilities across the trees that make up the forest. In many cases, finding the correct tuning parameters for a forest model can be quite tricky and time consuming. The autotuning options within PROC FOREST takes all of the guess work out of the tuning process and determines the optimal settings for these parameters based on the data. In this case, we allow PROC FOREST to autotune over the number of trees, the number of variables to try when splitting each node in the trees, and the in-bag fraction parameters for this model. We are using the outmodel option in this procedure to store all of the information about the model and to show an alternative to using score code. We can see mycaslib.forest_model being passed into the inmodel option within the second PROC FOREST call. This will be used to create our new output table containing our classifications for this model. Note that we could have specified the OUTPUT statement in the first PROC FOREST run because we are scoring the original input data. This approach would be used when you are scoring new data with the trained forest.

```
/* Autotune ntrees, vars_to_try and inbagfraction in Forest */
proc forest data=&prepped_data. intervalbins=20 minleafsize=5 seed=12345
outmodel=mycaslib.forest_model;
  input &interval_inputs. / level = interval;
  input &class_inputs. / level = nominal;
  target &target. / level=nominal;
  grow GAIN;
  partition rolevar=_partind_(train='1' validate='0');
  autotune maxiter=2 popsize=2 useparameters=custom
          tuneparms=(ntrees(lb=20 ub=100 init=100)
                     vars_to_try(init=5 lb=5 ub=20)
                     inbagfraction(init=0.6 lb=0.2 ub=0.9));
  ods output TunerResults=rf_tuner_results;
run;

/* Score the data using the generated Forest model */
proc forest data=&prepped_data. inmodel=mycaslib.forest_model noprint;
  output out=mycaslib._scored_FOREST copyvars=(b_tgt _partind_ account);
run;
```

In order to use this model in a different environment, such as in the next section where we use Python to build and compare models, the definition of this model must be promoted. For the Forest model, this definition was stored with the OUTMODEL option on the original PROC FOREST call creating the forest_model table. This promotion is done using PROC CASUTIL.

```
/* Promote the forest_model table */
proc casutil outcaslib="public" incaslib="public";
  promote casdata="forest_model";
quit;
```

Information about the autotuning process is shown in Figure 12. The Tuner Summary table details the optimization settings used to solve this problem. For example, the total tuning time of this model took 942.46 seconds with an Initial Objective Value of 7.3321 resulting in the Best Objective Value of 7.2532. The Best Configuration table shows that the optimal parameter settings for this data occurred at the second evaluation with 40 Trees, 11 Variables to Try, and a Bootstrap Sample (in-bag fraction) of 0.4027. Note that the misclassification for the validation partition is 0.0725.

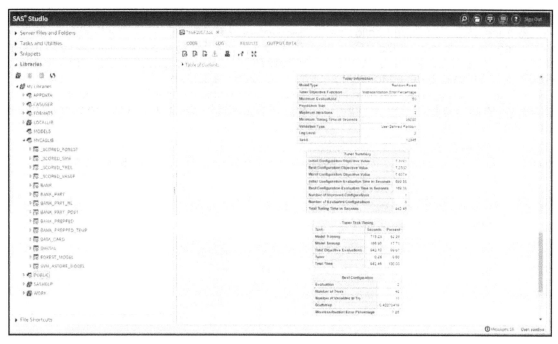

Figure 12. Forest Autotuning Metrics from SAS Studio

The final model that we will build is a Support Vector Machine. Support Vector Machines find a set of hyperplanes that best separate the levels of a binary target variable. We will use a polynomial kernel of degree 2 and store this complex model within a binary astore table called svm_astore_model. This table is then used in the PROC ASTORE call to generate the output table including your predicted classifications for this SVM model.

```
/* SUPPORT VECTOR MACHINE predictive model */
proc svmachine data=&prepped_data. (where=(_partind_=1));
  kernel polynom / deg=2;
  target &target. ;
  input &interval_inputs. / level=interval;
  input &class_inputs. / level=nominal;
  savestate rstore=mycaslib.svm_astore_model (promote=yes);
  ods exclude IterHistory;
run;


/* Score data using ASTORE code generated for the SVM model */
proc astore;
  score data=&prepped_data. out=mycaslib._scored_SVM
        rstore=mycaslib.svm_astore_model
        copyvars=(b_tgt _partind_  account);
run;

proc casutil outcaslib="public" incaslib="public";
  promote casdata="svm_astore_model";
quit;
```

Now that we have built several candidate models within SAS Studio, we want to compare these to each other to determine the best model for fitting this data. We also want to compare these with the original Gradient Boosting model, which was identified as the champion within SAS Visual Analytics. The details of this champion model were stored in an analytic store binary file and exported into the models library that is available within SAS Studio. To include this model in our comparisons, PROC ASTORE is run to apply this model to the BANK_PART data and to create the associated classifications.

```
proc casutil;
    Load casdata="Gradient_Boosting_VA.sashdat" incaslib="models"
    casout="gstate" outcaslib=casuser replace;
run;

data mycaslib.bank_part_post;
  set &partitioned_data.;
  _va_calculated_54_1=round('b_tgt'n,1.0);
  _va_calculated_54_2=round('demog_genf'n,1.0);
  _va_calculated_54_3=round('demog_ho'n,1.0);
  _va_calculated_54_4=round('_PartInd_'n,1.0);
run;

proc astore;
    score data=mycaslib.bank_part_post out=mycaslib._scored_vasgf
          rstore=casuser.gstate copyvars=(b_tgt _partind_ account ) ;
run;
```

These four candidate models are then passed to PROC ASSESS to calculate standard metrics including misclassification, lift, ROC, and more. Figure 13 shows that the best performing model for these candidates is the Forest model with a validation misclassification of 0.072532. This is also confirmed by looking at the ROC plot and the Lift values in the upper deciles.

```
/* Assess */
%macro assess_model(prefix=, var_evt=, var_nevt=);
  proc assess data=mycaslib._scored_&prefix.;
    input &var_evt.;
    target &target. / level=nominal event='1';
    fitstat pvar=&var_nevt. / pevent='0';
    by _partind_;

    ods output
      fitstat=&prefix._fitstat
      rocinfo=&prefix._rocinfo
      liftinfo=&prefix._liftinfo;
run;
%mend assess_model;

ods exclude all;
%assess_model(prefix=TREE, var_evt=p_b_tgt1, var_nevt=p_b_tgt0);
%assess_model(prefix=FOREST, var_evt=p_b_tgt1, var_nevt=p_b_tgt0);
%assess_model(prefix=SVM, var_evt=p_b_tgt1, var_nevt=p_b_tgt0);
%assess_model(prefix=VAGBM, var_evt=p_b_tgt1, var_nevt=p_b_tgt0);
ods exclude none;
```

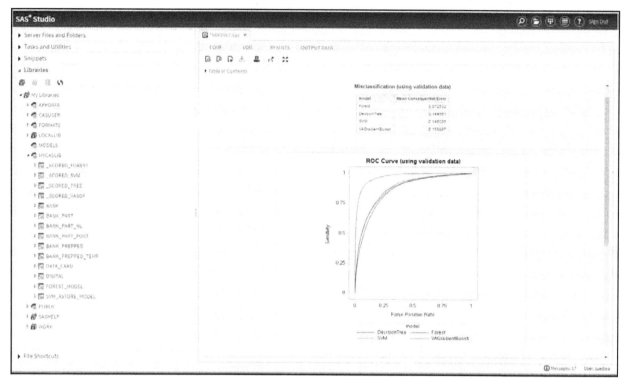

Figure 13. Assessment Statistics and ROC Curve for Candidate Models from SAS Studio

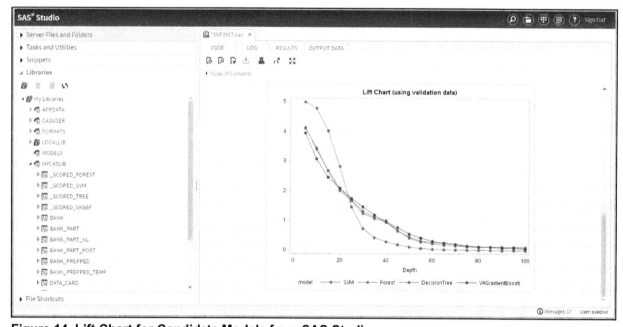

Figure 14. Lift Chart for Candidate Models from SAS Studio

BUILD MODEL PROGRAMMATICALLY USING PYTHON API

After exploring and modeling interactively in SAS Visual Analytics and programmatically in SAS Studio, we move into the open source world and finish this case study with another programmatic interface using the Python API. In this section, we will build a logistic regression model, score models that were built earlier in SAS Visual Analytics and SAS Studio, and compare them all to select a champion. The code and plots below are executed in Jupyter notebook.

We start by importing the SAS Scripting Wrapper for Analytics Transfer (SWAT) package to enable the connection and functionality of CAS. It is available at https://github.com/sassoftware/python-swat.

```
# Import packages
from swat import *
from pprint import pprint
from swat.render import render_html
from matplotlib import pyplot as plt
import pandas as pd
import sys
%matplotlib inline
```

The next step is to connect to CAS and start a new session. This step requires that you know the server host (cashost), port (casport), and authentication (casauth) of your CAS environment. Contact your SAS administrator for additional details and ensure that this code executes successfully before proceeding.

```
# Start a CAS session
cashost='cas_server_host.com'
casport=1234
casauth='~/_authinfo'
sess = CAS(cashost, casport, authinfo=casauth, caslib="public")
```

After execution, your CAS session can be accessed via the sess variable.

Next we define helper variables. Helper variables are those that are created in one place, at the beginning and reused afterward throughout the code. They include variables like the name of your input data set, its class and interval inputs, any shared caslibs, and so on.

```
# Set helper variables
gcaslib="public"
prepped_data="bank_prepped"
target = {"b_tgt"}
class_inputs = {"cat_input1", "cat_input2", "demog_ho", "demog_genf",
"demog_genm"}
interval_inputs = {"im_demog_age", "im_demog_homeval", "im_demog_inc",
"demog_pr", "log_rfm1", "rfm2", "log_im_rfm3", "rfm4", "rfm5", "rfm6",
"rfm7", "rfm8", "rfm9", "rfm10", "rfm11", "rfm12"}
class_vars = target | class_inputs
```

We begin by building a logistic regression model with stepwise selection, using the same set of inputs and target (b_tgt) used in the SAS Studio interface. Logistic regression models a binary target (0 or 1) and computes probabilities of the target event (1) as a function of specified inputs. This model uses the training partition of BANK_PREPPED table that was created and promoted to public caslib in SAS Studio. Because the table is promoted, it is available to any session on CAS, including ours.

After the model is run, the parameter estimates, fit statistics, and so on are displayed using render_html function from swat.render package. The Selection Summary in Figure 15 below lists the order of input variables selected at each step based on the SBC criterion. The misclassification rate for the validation partition is 0.1569. Finally, the predicted probabilities p_b_tgt0 and p_b_tgt1 are created using SAS DATA step code through the dataStep.runCode CAS action – these are needed later when invoking the model assessment function asses_model.

Note: Before invoking any CAS action, make sure the appropriate CAS actionset is loaded using sess.loadactionset. In the code below, notice that the regression actionset is loaded before the logistic action is invoked.

```
# Load action set
sess.loadactionset(actionset="regression")
```

```
# Train Logistic Regression
lr=sess.regression.logistic(
  table={"name":prepped_data, "caslib":gcaslib},
  classVars=[{"vars":class_vars}],
  model={
    "depVars":[{"name":"b_tgt", "options":{"event":"1"}}],
    "effects":[{"vars":class_inputs | interval_inputs}]
  },
  partByVar={"name":"_partind_", "train":"1", "valid":"0"},
  selection={"method":"STEPWISE"},
  output={"casOut":{"name":"_scored_logistic", "replace":True},
"copyVars":{"account", "b_tgt", "_partind_"}}
)

# Output model statistics
render_html(lr)

# Compute p_b_tgt0 and p_b_tgt1 for assessment
sess.dataStep.runCode(
  code="data _scored_logistic; set _scored_logistic; p_b_tgt0=1-_pred_;
rename _pred_=p_b_tgt1; run;"
)
```

Selection Summary					
Step	Effect Entered	Effect Removed	Number Of Effects	SBC	Optimal SBC
0	Intercept		1	736748.2097	0
1	rfm5		2	635388.82523	0
2	IM_demog_homeval		3	602525.74866	0
3	LOG_RFM1		4	565460.62424	0
4	rfm9		5	528458.08771	0
5	rfm12		6	525332.71656	0
6	cat_input1		7	523914.11582	0
7	cat_input2		8	522798.02005	0
8	rfm4		9	522395.70936	1

Figure 15. Selection Summary of Logistic Regression Model from Python API

After building a model using the Python API, let us score few models created in SAS Visual Analytics and SAS Studio to understand how a model created in one interface can be shared and reused in another. We will begin with the Gradient Boosting model created in SAS Visual DATA steps. When this model was built, it produced two artifacts: SAS data step code and an astore file that was saved to models caslib.

To score the Gradient Boosting model using these artifacts, the code does the following:
1. Loads the astore file into a local user caslib (casuser)
2. Runs SAS DATA step code created in SAS Visual Analytics – this transforms the input data set BANK_PREPPED with any necessary changes made within this interface
3. Scores the transformed input data set (from step 2) using the loaded astore file (from step 1) that contains model parameters
4. Renames predicted probability variable names for assessment

```
# 1. Load GBM model (ASTORE) created in VA
sess.loadTable(
    caslib="models", path="Gradient_Boosting_VA.sashdat",
    casout={"name":"gbm_astore_model","caslib":"casuser", "replace":True}
)

# 2. Score code from VA (for data preparation)
sess.dataStep.runCode(
    code="""data bank_part_post;
            set bank_part(caslib='public');
            _va_calculated_54_1=round('b_tgt'n,1.0);
            _va_calculated_54_2=round('demog_genf'n,1.0);
            _va_calculated_54_3=round('demog_ho'n,1.0);
            _va_calculated_54_4=round('_PartInd_'n,1.0);
        run;"""
)

# 3. Score using ASTORE
sess.loadactionset(actionset="astore")

sess.astore.score(
    table={"name":"bank_part_post"},
    rstore={"name":"gbm_astore_model"},
    out={"name":"_scored_gbm", "replace":True},
    copyVars={"account", "_partind_", "b_tgt"}
)

# 4. Rename p_b_tgt0 and p_b_tgt1 for assessment
sess.dataStep.runCode(
    code="""data _scored_gbm;
            set _scored_gbm;
            rename p__va_calculated_54_10=p_b_tgt0
                   p__va_calculated_54_11=p_b_tgt1;
        run;"""
)
```

We repeat the scoring process with the autotuned Forest model created in SAS Studio. Remember that this model was saved earlier as a CAS table called forest_model in the public caslib. Here the decisionTree.forestScore action scores the input data set BANK_PREPPED using the forest_model table. The SAS DATA step that follows creates the necessary predicted probability variable names for assessment.

```
# Load action set
sess.loadactionset(actionset="decisionTree")

# Score using forest_model table
sess.decisionTree.forestScore(
    table={"name":prepped_data, "caslib":gcaslib},
    modelTable={"name":"forest_model", "caslib":"public"},
    casOut={"name":"_scored_rf", "replace":True},
    copyVars={"account", "b_tgt", "_partind_"},
    vote="PROB"
)
```

```
# Create p_b_tgt0 and p_b_tgt1 as _rf_predp_ is the probability of event in
_rf_predname_
sess.dataStep.runCode(
  code="""data _scored_rf;
            set _scored_rf;
            if _rf_predname_=1 then do;
              p_b_tgt1=_rf_predp_;
              p_b_tgt0=1-p_b_tgt1;
            end;
            if _rf_predname_=0 then do;
              p_b_tgt0=_rf_predp_;
              p_b_tgt1=1-p_b_tgt0;
            end;
          run;"""
)
```

Lastly we score the Support Vector Machine model created in SAS Studio using the analytic store (astore) table svm_astore_model located in public caslib.

```
# Score using ASTORE
sess.loadactionset(actionset="astore")

sess.astore.score(
  table={"name":prepped_data, "caslib":gcaslib},
  rstore={"name":"svm_astore_model", "caslib":"public"},
  out={"name":"_scored_svm", "replace":True},
  copyVars={"account", "_partind_", "b_tgt"}
)
```

The final step in the case study is to assess and compare all of the models that were created and scored, including both the interactively and programmatically created models. The assessment is based on the validation partition of the data. The code below uses the percentile.assess action for Logistic Regression model but similar code can be used to generate assessments for all other models.

```
# Assess models
def assess_model(prefix):
    return sess.percentile.assess(
      table={
        "name":"_scored_" + prefix,
        "where": "strip(put(_partind_, best.))='0'"
      },
      inputs=[{"name":"p_b_tgt1"}],
      response="b_tgt",
      event="1",
      pVar={"p_b_tgt0"},
      pEvent={"0"}
    )

lrAssess=assess_model(prefix="logistic")
lr_fitstat =lrAssess.FitStat
lr_rocinfo =lrAssess.ROCInfo
lr_liftinfo=lrAssess.LIFTInfo
```

To choose a champion, we will use the ROC and Lift plots. Figures 16 and 17 shows that the autotuned Forest (SAS Studio) is the winner compared to the Logistic Regression (Python API), Support Vector

Machine (SAS Studio) and Gradient Boosting (SAS Visual Analytics) models as it has higher lift and more area under the ROC curve.

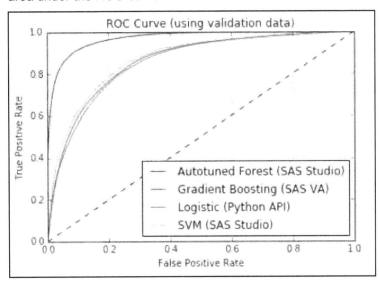

Figure 16. ROC Chart for Candidate Models

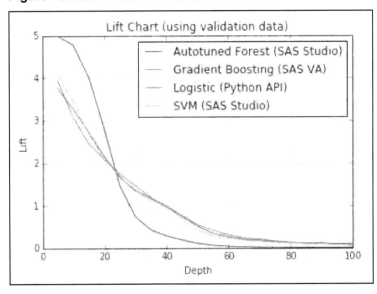

Figure 17. Lift Chart for Candidate Models

The goal of this case study is to highlight the unified and open architecture of SAS Viya -- how models built across various interfaces (SAS Visual Analytics, SAS Studio, and Python API) can seamlessly access data sets and intermediary results and easily score across them. Now that you understand the basics, you can build the best predictive model possible.

CONCLUSION

As previously stated, you should be able to solve business problems using your tool *and* method of choice, with no technological limitations. As shown in this paper, you can interactively build models quickly and accurately, and continue your analysis programmatically, without sacrificing inaccuracy from inefficient manual handoffs.

SAS Viya enables you to explore your data deeper, using the latest innovations in in-memory analytics. SAS is committed to delivering new, innovative data mining and machine learning algorithms that will scale to the size of your business, now and in the future.

REFERENCES

Koch, P., Wujek, B., Golovidov, O., and Gardner, S. (2017). "Automated Hyperparameter Tuning for Effective Machine Learning." In *Proceedings of the SAS Global Forum 2017 Conference*. Cary, NC: SAS Institute Inc.

ACKNOWLEDGMENTS

The authors express sincere gratitude to the SAS® Visual Data Mining and Machine Learning developers, testers, and also to our customers.

RECOMMENDED READING AND ASSETS

- SAS Visual Analytics, SAS Visual Statistics, and SAS Visual Data Mining and Machine Learning 8.1 on SAS Viya: Video Library (Visual)
  http://support.sas.com/training/tutorial/viyava/

- SAS Visual Data Mining and Machine Learning on SAS Viya: Video Library (Programming)
  http://support.sas.com/training/tutorial/viya/index.html

- SAS Visual Data Mining and Machine Learning Fact Sheet
  http://www.sas.com/content/dam/SAS/en_us/doc/factsheet/sas-visual-data-mining-machine-learning-1082751.pdf

- SAS Visual Data Mining and Machine Learning Community
  https://communities.sas.com/t5/SAS-Visual-Data-Mining-and/bd-p/dmml

- SAS Viya Documentation
  http://support.sas.com/documentation/onlinedoc/viya/

- SAS Software Github Page
  https://github.com/sassoftware

CONTACT INFORMATION

Your comments and questions are valued and encouraged. Contact the author at:

Jonathan Wexler
SAS Institute Inc.
100 SAS Campus Drive
Cary, NC 27513
Email: jonathan.wexler@sas.com

Susan Haller
SAS Institute Inc.
100 SAS Campus Drive
Cary, NC 27513
Email: susan.haller@sas.com

Radhikha Myneni
SAS Institute Inc.
100 SAS Campus Drive
Cary, NC 27513
Email: radhikha.myneni@sas.com

Counter Radicalization through Investigative Insights and Data Exploitation Using SAS® Viya™

Lawrie Elder, SAS Institute Inc.

ABSTRACT

This end-to-end capability demonstration illustrates how SAS Viya can aid intelligence, homeland security, and law-enforcement agencies in counterterrorism activities. Many of us are familiar with recent examples of agency failure to apportion significance to isolated pieces of information that, in context, are indicative of an escalating threat, and that require intervention. Recent terrorist acts have been carried out by radicalized individuals who should have been firmly on the organizational radar. Although SAS products perform analysis and interpretation of data that enables the law enforcement and homeland security communities to recognize and triage threats, intelligence information must be viewed in its full context. SAS Viya can rationalize previously disconnected capabilities in a single platform, empowering intelligence, security, and law enforcement agencies. SAS® Visual Investigator functions as a hub for SAS® Event Stream Processing, SAS® Visual Scenario Designer, and SAS® Visual Analytics, combining network analysis, triage, and, by leveraging the mobile capability of SAS, operational case management to drive insights, leads, and investigation. This hub provides the capability to ingest social media data, and to cross-reference both internally held data and, crucially, operational intelligence gained from normal policing activities. This presentation chronicles the exposure and substantiation of a radical network and describes tactical and strategic disruption.

INTRODUCTION

This paper begins with an overview of the terrorist threat currently faced by the European and Transatlantic communities and then explains how SAS capabilities can support agencies engaged in counterterrorism efforts. While acknowledging that the origins and nature of current terrorism threats vary significantly, this paper focuses primarily on the Salafist (radical Sunni) extremist threat.

Environment and History

Recent military success against Salafi jihadist terrorist groups has seen the Islamic State in Iraq and the Levant (ISIL) losing their foothold in territories that have been considered the heartlands of Iraq and Syria. A notable consequence of these developments has been a strengthening of these groups' commitment to target Europe and North America. This approach has met with some success, drawing on the experience of European ISIL fighters returning from the frontlines. Simultaneously, they have set out to motivate "lone-wolf" activities by developing localized networks of extremists through the use of propaganda.

These ISIL activities have driven several recent high-profile, high-casualty attacks, primarily against European civilian targets in heavily populated public areas. Their tactics have varied greatly, ranging from sophisticated, highly coordinated attacks to crude, blunt-force strikes. Perhaps more significantly, these attacks have served to highlight failings in the local, national, and international intelligence and enforcement services who are perceived to have missed opportunities to preemptively disrupt them.

The changing nature of the terrorist threat has required intelligence and enforcement agencies to shift their focus and adjust their tactics. Perhaps the greatest influence on this change has been that recent attacks have been largely perpetrated by individuals who have subsequently been revealed to be known criminals. Indeed, many of ISIL's successes can be directly attributed to this ability to radicalize individuals whose history has previously been marked by petty crime.

These factors are driving changes in the counterterrorism dynamic and have exposed weaknesses in the traditional capabilities around gathering, exploiting, and sharing of intelligence within and between agencies and nations. While counterterrorism has traditionally been the domain of intelligence and homeland security agencies, recent terrorist attacks (born out of and planned within criminal networks) have to a large extent ranged beyond these services' purview. This change in dynamic has placed law enforcement at the center of counterterrorism endeavors and has, as a direct consequence, seen general policing or community information elevated to being among the most critical of data sources.

Examples

Sophisticated and Coordinated: In November 2015 a brutal, highly coordinated attack took place in Paris when ISIL-inspired terrorist cells, using assault rifles and wearing suicide vests, simultaneously attacked multiple soft targets, including the Bataclan Theatre, where 89 died. The terrorist network behind the attack was led by Salah Abdesalam, a radicalized individual with strong links to known criminal networks. The group also included individuals who had previously fought in Syria.

Michael Leiter, former director of the United States' National Counterterrorism Center, commented afterward that "the attacks demonstrated a sophistication not seen in a city attack since the 2008 Mumbai attacks, and would change how the West regards the threat" of terrorism generally.

Blunt Force: In July 2016 Mohamed Lahouaiej Bouhlel drove a lorry into a Bastille Day celebration in Nice, France, killing 84 people. This blunt-force attack might have lacked the sophistication and planning of the Paris attack, but it ultimately had a similarly deadly effect. Although Bouhlel was known to law enforcement for involvement in petty criminality, there were no reports of his having any direct links with a terrorist group. However, he was subsequently described by ISIL as a "soldier of Islam." Significantly, he was known to have psychiatric problems, a characteristic increasingly common in these incidents.

The evidence indicated that Bouhlel had been radicalized by ISIL propaganda, and he was subsequently classified by elements of the mainstream media as a "lone-wolf" actor. Nevertheless, he did not act alone in the planning and development of his attack, and his actions were facilitated by criminal contacts through which, among other activities, he procured a firearm.

Future

Transatlantic law-enforcement communities have publicly acknowledged their current weaknesses and their vulnerability to future terrorist attacks. This recognition has resulted in a number of initiatives to assist with building understanding of possible ways to mitigate such threats in the future.

A significant body of work is to be found in the GLOBSEC Intelligence Reform Initiative (GRI), which recently published a paper, "Reforming Transatlantic Counter-Terrorism". One of the important observations of this paper was the following:

> *"The key problem the Globsec Intelligence Reform Initiative addresses is that of intelligence and personal data sharing and its operationalisation at the domestic as well as transnational level. Although many intelligence agencies have been at the centre of counter-terrorism efforts since 9/11, this report recognises that as terrorism is fundamentally viewed as a crime in both Europe and North America, law enforcement is increasingly at the centre of better pan-European and transatlantic counter-terrorism cooperation. Crucially, better fusion of intelligence processes, and intelligence and law enforcement agencies, is needed to provide the means for pre-empting terrorist attacks before they occur, rather than relying on effective investigation after the event."*

While the need for data sharing and the operationalization of intelligence products is widely accepted, there is also a recognition that to be effective, agencies must enhance the information technology capabilities around collation, analysis, and the associated management of operational processes.

The related significant challenges are often magnified rather than lessened by the volume of data that exists for agencies to exploit. Information sources are vast and varied, a complexity that is only increased by this now essential inclusion of day-to-day community and policing data.

SAS VIYA PLATFORM

Supported by SAS Data Management services, the SAS Viya platform can help law enforcement, security, and intelligence agencies to address the many challenges associated with counterterrorism. SAS Viya comprises solutions built with embedded analytical capabilities at their core, allowing the exploitation of information through alerting, triage, enrichment, and operationalization. The open architecture of SAS Viya also ensures that operatives at all levels within participating organizations (including executives, analysts, investigators, and front-line officers) are always able to access their data and related insights in the most effective and relevant manner and are not tied to a single application or device.

With SAS Viya, it is possible to integrate all aspects of the intelligence and investigation life cycles through standard, unified components that provide a foundation for sharing and communicating. The major components of such a system to handle data for intelligence purposes would include (but not be limited to) the following SAS solutions:

- SAS® Visual Analytics
- SAS® Event Stream Processing
- SAS® Mobile Investigator
- SAS® Visual Investigator

SAS VISUAL ANALYTICS

Business Challenge

In tackling the terrorist threat, law enforcement, security, and intelligence agencies must use their finite resources to the best possible effect. Decisions must be based on accurate assessments, and the strategic direction must always be made clear and be justifiable.

The development of an effective Strategic Assessment is dependent on skilled operatives' undertaking detailed research and analysis of all available information sources. To develop this "big-picture" document and truly understand the nature and level of the threats, agencies should not restrict their information sources to only those that are routinely maintained or accessed in the course of day-to-day operations. External influences, such as information about public perceptions, health, welfare, and education, must also be taken into consideration, as such factors can provide valuable insight into the fears, vulnerabilities, and threats extant in local communities.

By making a comprehensive and complete assessment available, agencies are better able to set a strategic direction, prioritize, make defensible decisions, and allocate resources intelligently, fully considering the operational options available to them. Counter-radicalization is a related priority, and agencies must take all necessary actions to understand the terrorist ideology, identify those who promote it, and prevent people from being drawn into terrorism. Tactical options when seeking to prevent radicalization or to preempt a terrorist attack would include proactive investigation, surveillance, education, and engaging with sectors and institutions where the risks of radicalization are greatest.

This practice of centering activity on a strategic assessment is universal among the European and Transatlantic law-enforcement, security, and intelligence agencies, and this commonality facilitates collaboration on an interagency, national, and international basis. There are many examples where this type of joint assessment has been adopted: for example, a joint endeavor of the European Council to develop the EU Counter-Terrorism Strategy[1]

---

[1] http://www.consilium.europa.eu/en/policies/fight-against-terrorism/.

Applicable SAS Viya Module

SAS Visual Analytics supports agencies in creating, sharing, and acting upon interactive and meaningful intelligence products, such as strategic assessments.

By using SAS Visual Analytics, analysts gain the ability to explore the corpus of information available within the organization as well as that shared through collaboration. Products will include the vital and overarching strategic assessment, together with tactical reports reflecting priorities and supporting ongoing operations.

Given the dynamic nature of the terrorist threat, the interactive features of SAS Visual Analytics reports are crucial. These reports enable recipients to focus on the information facets that are most appropriate and in whatever manner is most relevant to the task at hand, using filters and drill-through capabilities to further explore the data and develop insights.

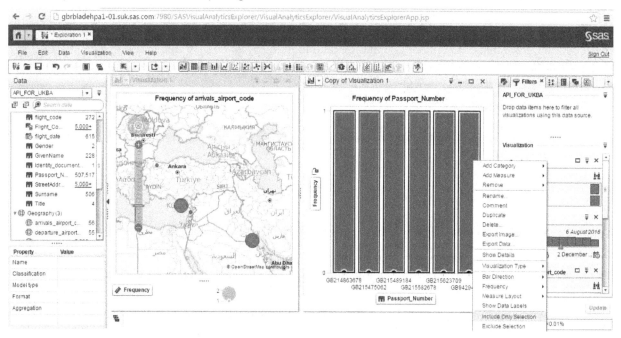

Figure 1. Example of SAS Visual Analytics dashboard

A standard response to a terrorist incident will see different levels of commanders taking control of the various aspects of activity (for example, overall command, referred to as Gold; tactical: Silver; and operational: Bronze). SAS Visual Analytics gives commanders easy access to explore dashboards and reports to aid in their decision-making process. The ability to access this information from mobile devices is of particular importance to bronze commanders who are often required to operate from the field (for example, taking responsibility for hostage situations or bomb scene management).

SAS EVENT STREAM PROCESSING

Business Challenge

There is an expectation--however unrealistic--that law enforcement and intelligence agencies have the capability to manage and exploit (at least in some form) **all** of the information sources held by or made available to them. However, even within a single organization data management can be challenging, as disparate information sets are often held in discrete "silos" – with different schemas, access rights, and organizational practices. Multi-agency collaboration only serves to increase this potential complexity, leaving practitioners with the task of interpreting significant quantities of ever-changing information, presented in a variety of ways. By adding layers of third-party, high-volume data sources (such as communications data or automatic license plate recognition data), the challenge only increases almost exponentially.

The limitation of software tools that have previously been available to agencies is that they may only be able to exploit available information after the event. An analysis of circumstances surrounding recent terror attacks would seem to indicate that investigators were unaware of critical information that was already held by their organization, which might therefore be seen to have missed opportunities for preemptive action. Inevitably, starting an investigation after an event has occurred leaves analysts and investigators playing catch-up as they try to keep pace with new investigative streams and evolving events.

Applicable SAS Viya Module

SAS Event Stream Processing can support agencies in addressing the challenges presented by the attempt to keep up with such potentially vast quantities of information by applying analytics to the data as it becomes available.

With SAS Event Stream Processing, huge volumes of data streaming in real time from multiple jurisdictions, organizations, and nations can be filtered, categorized, aggregated, and cleansed before being stored, saving operatives from having to sort through and interpret disconnected and often polluted data sources.

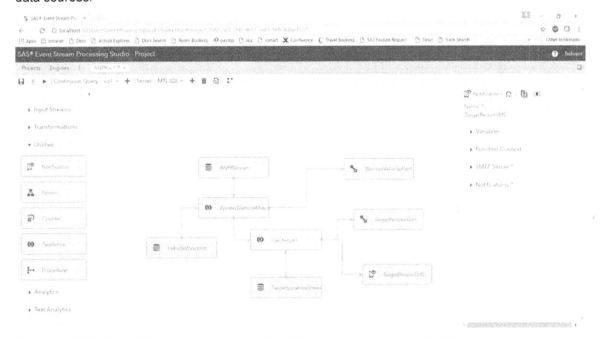

Figure 2. SAS Event Stream Processing identifying vehicle on watch list

SAS Event Stream Processing is a powerful tool that is capable of enhancing an organization's capacity to respond to emerging threats and take preemptive action. It can apply analytical models simultaneously to both fast-moving and static data, ensuring that relevant information is isolated and that analysts receive timely alerts related to significant events; identified criminal networks and activity; or anomalous behavior.

As an example: An alert is generated by two seemingly unconnected individuals traveling separately to a country with known affiliation to terrorism, their travel being paid for using the same credit card.

While alerts to items of significance are of great value, organizations are further challenged with converting such insights into operational action.

SAS MOBILE INVESTIGATOR

Business Challenge

The previously discussed acceptance that community and general policing data is now essential to the counterterrorism effort has exposed the weaknesses in existing systems. In most nations, the responsibility for the individual facets of such "day-to-day" policing is managed by distinct departments or units, potentially even split across multiple agencies or organizations (for example, road traffic, community policing, or criminal investigation units). An unfortunate--but natural--consequence of this reality has been that vital data is held in disparate stores, and with the limitations of legacy software, there is often no simple means to search across, rationalize, or identify information of significance within these "siloed" repositories.

While this situation is generally most prevalent among law enforcement agencies, similar architectural and functional challenges exist within the wider intelligence and security communities. The need for the modernization of systems is widespread, as these agencies seek to increase their access to and their exploitation of the data available to them.

Of particular note is a recognized need to improve the ability to obtain intelligence as quickly as possible ("fast time intelligence") in the aftermath of a significant event. Weakness in this area was clearly evidenced in reviews of the post-incident responses of law-enforcement agencies to many of the recent European attacks. And while there is no argument that officers responding to those incidents deserve the highest praise, their actions would undoubtedly have been hampered by inevitable delays in identifying crucial investigative leads within such disconnected information stores.

Applicable SAS Viya Module

SAS Mobile Investigator is designed to meet the specific needs of intelligence, enforcement, and investigative agencies. It provides a comprehensive operational environment capable of supporting the nuanced processes of intelligence and law-enforcement agencies–an environment that is essential to ensure legislative and regulatory compliance–through key capabilities such as advanced search; tasking; operational reporting; a robust configurable security model; and comprehensive auditing.

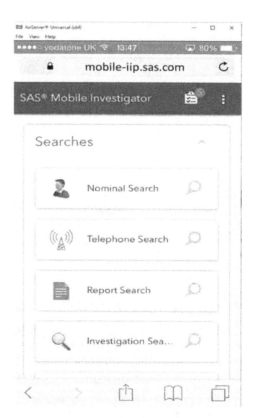

SAS Mobile Investigator is a web-based application that uses responsive design to alter the ways that the various components are presented, ensuring that all functionality is easily available on whatever type of device is used to access the system (for example, mobile, desktop, and so on). Further, this design enables the capabilities of each device to be used as appropriate. For example, a user accessing the system via a mobile phone would be able to use the GPS capabilities of the device to log the precise location of an incident, and use the camera to capture an image or video, which could be immediately uploaded and made available.

While seemingly straightforward, the value associated with this type of mobile access cannot be overstated. Officers in the field can receive tasks, comply with due process, and upload what could prove to be invaluable information without having to return to an office or to a vehicle.

Figure 3: SAS Mobile Investigator

The enabling of officers to feed "street-level" intelligence directly into the corpus of knowledge about a particular individual, group, or community will enhance the agencies' ability to spot behavioral patterns and anomalies, perhaps indicative of changing social dynamics, and to prioritize appropriate intervention, for example, investigation, education, or disruption.

Having field access to the totality of organizational data allows officers (in near real time) to review information relevant to live incidents, assess risks, and customize their responses appropriately while remaining cognizant of the "bigger picture". While these capabilities are clearly important for ongoing investigations and routine operational activity, the ability to facilitate fast time intelligence gathering and exchange of information in the immediate aftermath of a terrorist incident could prove crucial in facilitating early arrests, or preempting further attacks.

SAS VISUAL INVESTIGATOR

Business Challenge

The working practices of intelligence and law enforcement communities have evolved over many years and are generally well defined, reflecting the needs and priorities of individual organizations and their practitioners. These practices might still be valid today, but they must now be applied against the modern environment where the volume, variety, and velocity of data have reached unprecedented (and continually increasing) levels. In meeting these challenges, agencies require modern analytical tools that are able to refine and offer focus on relevant data while also supporting existing operational practices, so essential for intelligence development, for information sharing, and for ensuring the integrity of evidence collection.

Successful outcomes are often dependent on the early identification of factors that signify risk and require prioritization. These could include, for example, patterns within the data identifying known criminal networks, or a collection of (sometimes related; sometimes seemingly disparate) elements that indicate escalating risk. A real life example relating to the Salafi jihadist threat would be a pattern of actions, travel, communications, and lifestyle changes known to be a precursor to radicalization.

Applicable SAS Viya Module

SAS Visual Investigator provides an environment where operatives can–through the processes of alert generation, search, and the application of advanced analytics--work on and keep pace with the volume and variety of data that is now available to be exploited. Similar to SAS Mobile Investigator, SAS Visual Investigator supports (and where required, enforces) the nuances of operational process that are required for legislative and regulatory compliance.

As the nature of terrorist threats evolves, agencies will be required to adjust their focus to seek out objects and patterns within their data that could be of significance and require action. Alert generation through the application of rules and algorithms can highlight items of interest and, where possible, support early intervention.

Importantly, the graphical scenario builder feature in SAS Visual Investigator gives agencies the flexibility to address changing threats by designing, testing, and iterating rules that can automatically generate alerts on matching patterns within the data. This process can generate an alert based on the identification of a range of factors that, in isolation, might seem unrelated or of little significance, but when viewed as a whole, could be indicative of an escalating risk. For example, analysis might identify a pattern of behavioral factors, travel, and communications that could be associated with radicalization.

Scenarios that are designed within SAS Visual Investigator can also be enhanced using SAS Event Stream Processing to generate alerts from volume data in motion.

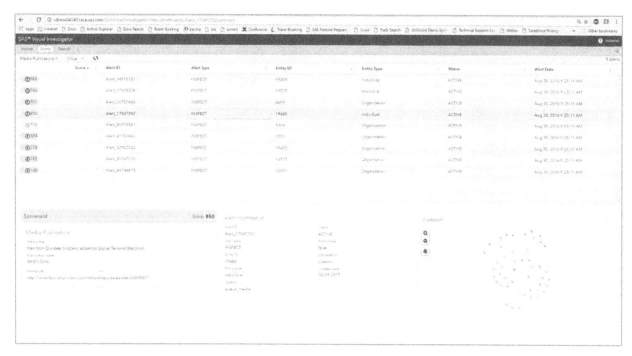

Figure 4. Example of SAS Visual Investigator alert management dashboard

The operationalization of data (including analytically derived alerts) is of paramount importance in counterterrorism efforts. SAS Visual Investigator supports triage, prioritization, and assignment of responsibility. Advanced analytical capabilities allow agencies to develop intelligence insights and uncover investigative streams.

In addition, insights that are derived from the data (such as network diagrams, timelines, or map views) can be used to create operational products that are essential to advance the work of agencies. For example, the data in SAS Visual Investigator can be used in the development of subject profiles, target packages, or threat assessments.

Crucially, data that is managed and developed within SAS Visual Investigator will be accessible through SAS Mobile Investigator, enabling officers to conduct research while in the field and receive tasks stemming from deskbound research.

Figure 5. SAS Visual Investigator network diagrams, map views

CONCLUSION

The European and Transatlantic intelligence, security, and law-enforcement agencies are well aware of the changes and improvements required to be successful in meeting the real and growing threat of terrorism. While significant progress has been made in international and interagency collaboration, clear weaknesses remain.

It is widely accepted that organizational disconnects can exist in all areas and at every level of an agency and are regularly manifested in ineffective communication between stakeholders and an inability to fully exploit the available information assets.

The magnitude of the counterterrorism challenge cannot be overstated. While there is no "magic bullet" to solve the problems that global terror poses, SAS Viya represents a unique opportunity to work toward the much needed cohesion in approach and to build on the existing corporate knowledge of the threat. In a single platform, SAS Viya offers a comprehensive set of capabilities to manage huge volumes of data while simultaneously facilitating strategic and operational activities through a combination of advanced analytics and business process support.

REFERENCES

GLOBSEC Intelligence Reform Initiative - Reforming Transatlantic Counter-Terrorism

(http://www.cepolicy.org/sites/cepolicy.org/files/attachments/giri_report_1.pdf)

European Council to develop the EU Counter-Terrorism Strategy
(http://www.consilium.europa.eu/en/policies/fight-against-terrorism/)

CONTACT INFORMATION

Your comments and questions are valued and encouraged. Contact the author at:

Lawrie Elder
SAS Investigation and Intelligence Practice
lawrie.elder@sas.com

SAS514-2017

Automated Hyperparameter Tuning for Effective Machine Learning

Patrick Koch, Brett Wujek, Oleg Golovidov, and Steven Gardner

SAS Institute Inc.

ABSTRACT

Machine learning predictive modeling algorithms are governed by "hyperparameters" that have no clear defaults agreeable to a wide range of applications. The *depth* of a decision tree, *number of trees* in a forest, *number of hidden layers* and *neurons in each layer* in a neural network, and *degree of regularization* to prevent overfitting are a few examples of quantities that must be prescribed for these algorithms. Not only do ideal settings for the hyperparameters dictate the performance of the training process, but more importantly they govern the quality of the resulting predictive models. Recent efforts to move from a manual or random adjustment of these parameters include rough grid search and intelligent numerical optimization strategies.

This paper presents an automatic tuning implementation that uses local search optimization for tuning hyperparameters of modeling algorithms in SAS® Visual Data Mining and Machine Learning. The AUTOTUNE statement in the TREESPLIT, FOREST, GRADBOOST, NNET, SVMACHINE, and FACTMAC procedures defines tunable parameters, default ranges, user overrides, and validation schemes to avoid overfitting. Given the inherent expense of training numerous candidate models, the paper addresses efficient distributed and parallel paradigms for training and tuning models on the SAS® Viya™ platform. It also presents sample tuning results that demonstrate improved model accuracy and offers recommendations for efficient and effective model tuning.

INTRODUCTION

Machine learning is a form of self-calibration of predictive models that are built from training data. Machine learning predictive modeling algorithms are commonly used to find hidden value in big data. Facilitating effective decision making requires the transformation of relevant data to high-quality descriptive and predictive models. The transformation presents several challenges however. For example, consider a neural network, as shown in Figure 1. Outputs are predicted by transforming a set of inputs through a series of hidden layers that are defined by activation functions linked with weights. Determining the activation functions and the weights to determine the best model configuration is a complex optimization problem.

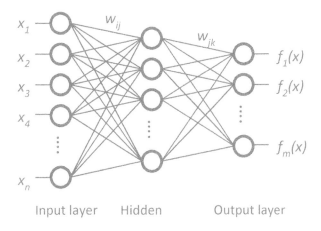

Figure 1. Neural Network

The goal in this model-training optimization problem is to find the weights that will minimize the error in model predictions based on the training data, validation data, specified model configuration (number of hidden layers and number of neurons in each hidden layer), and the level of regularization that is added to reduce overfitting to training data. One recently popular approach to solving for the weights in this optimization problem is through use of a *stochastic gradient descent* (SGD) algorithm (Bottou, Curtis, and Nocedal 2016). This algorithm is a variation of gradient descent in which instead of calculating the gradient of the loss over all observations to update the weights at each step, a "mini-batch" random sample of the observations is used to estimate loss, sampling without replacement until all observations have been used. The performance of this algorithm, as with all optimization algorithms, depends on a number of control parameters for which no default values are best for all problems. SGD parameters include the following control parameters (among others):

- a *learning rate* that controls the step size for selecting new weights

- a *momentum* parameter to avoid slow oscillations

- an *adaptive decay rate* and an *annealing rate* to adjust the learning rate for each weight and time

- a *mini-batch* size for sampling a subset of observations

The best values of the control parameters must be chosen very carefully. For example, the learning rate can be adjusted to reach a solution more quickly; however, if the value is too high, the solution diverges, and if it is too low, the performance is very slow, as shown in Figure 2(a). The momentum parameter dictates whether the algorithm tends to oscillate slowly in ravines where solutions lie (jumping back and forth across the ravine) or dives in quickly, as shown in Figure 2(b). But if momentum is too high, it could jump past the solution (Sutskever et al. 2013). Similar accuracy-versus-performance trade-offs are encountered with the other control parameters. The adaptive decay can be adjusted to improve accuracy, and the annealing rate is often necessary to avoid jumping past a solution. Ideally, the size of the mini-batch for distributed training is small enough to improve performance and large enough to produce accurate models. A communication frequency parameter can be used to adjust how often training information (such as average weights, velocity vectors, and annealing rates) is synced when training is distributed across a compute grid; higher frequency might increase accuracy, but it also reduces performance.

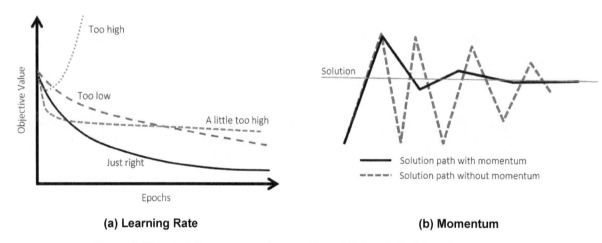

(a) Learning Rate   (b) Momentum

Figure 2. Effect of Hyperparameters on Neural Network Training Convergence

The best values of these parameters vary for different data sets, and they must be chosen before model training begins. These options dictate not only the performance of the training process, but more importantly, the quality of the resulting model. Because these parameters are external to the training process—that is, they are not the model parameters (weights in the neural network) being optimized during training—they are often called *hyperparameters*. Figure 3 depicts the distinction between *training* a model (solving for model parameters) and *tuning* a model (finding the best algorithm hyperparameter values). Settings for these hyperparameters can significantly influence the resulting accuracy of the predictive models, and there are no clear defaults that work well for different data sets. In addition to the optimization options already discussed for the SGD algorithm, the machine learning algorithms themselves have many hyperparameters. As in the neural network example, the *number of hidden layers*, the *number of neurons in each hidden layer*, the *distribution used for the initial weights*, and so on are all hyperparameters that are specified up front for model training, that govern the quality of the resulting model, and whose ideal values also vary widely with different data sets.

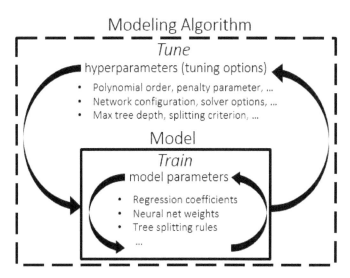

Figure 3. Model Training in Relation to Model Tuning

Tuning hyperparameter values is a critical aspect of the model training process and is considered a best practice for a successful machine learning application (Wujek, Hall, and Güneş 2016). The remainder of this paper describes some of the common traditional approaches to hyperparameter tuning and introduces a new hybrid approach in SAS Visual Data Mining and Machine Learning that takes advantage of the combination of the powerful machine learning algorithms, optimization routines, and distributed and parallel computing that running on the SAS Viya platform offers.

HYPERPARAMETER TUNING

The approach to finding the ideal values for hyperparameters (tuning a model to a particular data set) has traditionally been a manual effort. For guidance in setting these values, researchers often rely on their past experience using these machine learning algorithms to train models. However, even with expertise in machine learning algorithms and their hyperparameters, the best settings of these hyperparameters will change with different data; it is difficult to prescribe the hyperparameter values based on previous experience. The ability to explore alternative configurations in a more guided and automated manner is needed.

COMMON APPROACHES

Grid Search

A typical approach to exploring alternative model configurations is by using what is commonly known as a grid search. Each hyperparameter of interest is discretized into a desired set of values to be studied, and models are trained and assessed for all combinations of the values across all hyperparameters (that is, a "grid"). Although fairly simple and straightforward to carry out, a grid search is quite costly because expense grows exponentially with the number of hyperparameters and the number of discrete levels of each. Even with the inherent ability of a grid search to train and assess all candidate models in parallel (assuming an appropriate environment in which to do so), it must be quite coarse in order to be feasible, and thus it will often fail to identify an improved model configuration. Figure 4(a) illustrates hypothetical distributions of two hyperparameters (X_1 and X_2) with respect to a training objective and depicts the difficulty of finding a good combination with a coarse standard grid search.

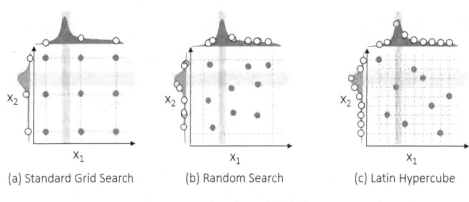

(a) Standard Grid Search   (b) Random Search   (c) Latin Hypercube

● = Individual model training and assessment

Figure 4. Common Approaches to Hyperparameter Tuning

Random Search

A simple yet surprisingly effective alternative to performing a grid search is to train and assess candidate models by using random combinations of hyperparameter values. As demonstrated in Bergstra and Bengio (2012), given the disparity in the sensitivity of model accuracy to different hyperparameters, a set of candidates that incorporates a larger number of trial values for each hyperparameter will have a much greater chance of finding effective values for each hyperparameter. Because some of the hyperparameters might actually have little to no effect on the model for certain data sets, it is prudent to avoid wasting the effort to evaluate all combinations, especially for higher-dimensional hyperparameter spaces. Rather than focusing on studying a full-factorial combination of all hyperparameter values, studying random combinations enables you to explore more values of each hyperparameter at the same cost (the number of candidate models that are trained and assessed). Figure 4(b) depicts a potential random distribution with the same budget of evaluations (nine points in this example) as shown for the grid search in Figure 4(a), highlighting the potential to find better hyperparameter values. Still, the effectiveness of evaluating purely random combinations of hyperparameter values is subject to the size and uniformity of the sample; candidate combinations can be concentrated in regions that completely omit the most effective values of one or more of the hyperparameters.

Latin Hypercube Sampling

A similar but more structured approach is to use a random Latin hypercube sample (LHS) (McKay 1992), an experimental design in which samples are exactly uniform across each hyperparameter but random in combinations. These so-called low-discrepancy point sets attempt to ensure that points are approximately equidistant from one another in order to fill the space efficiently. This sampling allows for coverage across the entire range of each hyperparameter and is more likely to find good values of each hyperparameter—as shown in Figure 4(c)—which can then be used to identify good combinations. Other experimental design procedures can also be quite effective at ensuring equal density sampling throughout the entire hyperparameter space, including optimal Latin hypercube sampling as proposed by Sacks et al. (1989).

Optimization

Exploring alternative model configurations by evaluating a discrete sample of hyperparameter combinations, whether randomly chosen or through a more structured experimental design approach, is certainly a fairly straightforward approach. However, true hyperparameter optimization should allow the use of logic and information from previously evaluated configurations to determine how to effectively search through the space. Discrete samples are unlikely to identify even a local accuracy peak or error valley in the hyperparameter space; searching between these discrete samples can uncover good combinations of hyperparameter values. The search is based on an objective of minimizing the model validation error, so each "evaluation" from the optimization algorithm's perspective is a full cycle of model training and validation. These methods are designed to make intelligent use of fewer evaluations and thus save on the overall computation time. Optimization algorithms that have been used for hyperparameter tuning include Broyden-Fletcher-Goldfarb-Shanno (BFGS) (Konen et al. 2011), covariance matrix adaptation evolution strategy (CMA-ES) (Konen et al. 2011), particle swarm (PS) (Renukadevi and Thangaraj 2014; Gomes et al. 2012), tabu search (TS) (Gomes et al. 2012), genetic algorithms (GA) (Lorena and de Carvalho 2008), and more recently surrogate-based Bayesian optimization (Denwancker et al. 2016).

However, because machine learning training and scoring algorithms are a complex black box to the tuning algorithm, they create a challenging class of optimization problems. **Figure 5** illustrates several of these challenges:

- Machine learning algorithms typically include not only continuous variables but also categorical and integer variables. These variables can lead to very discrete changes in the objective.

- In some cases, the hyperparameter space is discontinuous and the objective evaluation fails.

- The space can also be very noisy and nondeterministic (for example, when distributed data are moved around because of unexpected rebalancing).

- Objective evaluations can fail because a compute node fails, which can derail a search strategy.

- Often the space contains many flat regions where many configurations produce very similar models.

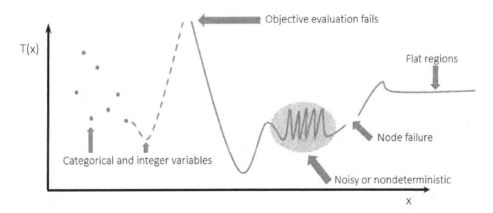

Figure 5. Challenges in Applying Optimization to Hyperparameter Tuning

An additional challenge is the unpredictable computation expense of training and validating predictive models using different hyperparameter values. For example, adding hidden layers and neurons to a neural network can significantly increase the training and validation time, resulting in widely ranging potential objective expense. Given the great promise of using intelligent optimization techniques coupled with the aforementioned challenges of applying these techniques for tuning machine learning hyperparameters, a very flexible and efficient search strategy is needed.

SAS Viya is a new platform that enables parallel/distributed computing of the powerful analytics that SAS provides. The new SAS Visual Data Mining and Machine Learning offering (Wexler, Haller, and Myneni 2017) provides a hyperparameter autotuning capability that is built on local search optimization in SAS® software. Optimization for hyperparameter tuning typically can very quickly reduce, by several percentage points, the model error that is produced by default settings of these hyperparameters. More advanced and extensive optimization, facilitated through parallel tuning to explore more configurations and refine hyperparameter values, can lead to further improvement. With increased dimensionality of the hyperparameter space (that is, as more hyperparameters require tuning), a manual tuning process becomes much more difficult and a much coarser grid search is required. An automated, parallelized search strategy can also benefit novice machine learning algorithm users.

LOCAL SEARCH OPTIMIZATION

SAS local search optimization (LSO) is a hybrid derivative-free optimization framework that operates in the SAS Viya parallel/distributed environment to overcome the challenges and expense of hyperparameter optimization. As shown in Figure 6, it consists of an extendable suite of search methods that are driven by a hybrid solver manager that controls concurrent execution of search methods. Objective evaluations (different model configurations in this case) are distributed across multiple evaluation worker nodes in a compute grid and coordinated in a feedback loop that supplies data from all concurrent running search methods. The strengths of this approach include handling of continuous, integer, and categorical variables; handling nonsmooth, discontinuous spaces; and ease of parallelizing the search strategy.

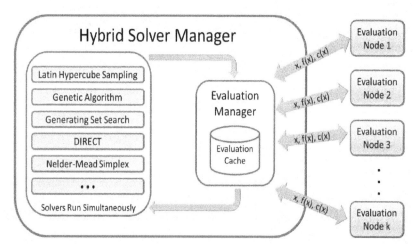

Figure 6. Local Search Optimization: Parallel Hybrid Derivative-Free Optimization Strategy

The autotuning capability in SAS Visual Data Mining and Machine Learning takes advantage of the LSO framework to provide a flexible and effective hybrid search strategy. It uses a default hybrid search strategy that begins with a Latin hypercube sample (LHS), which provides a more uniform sample of the hyperparameter space than a grid or random search provides. The best samples from the LHS are then used to seed a genetic algorithm (GA), which crosses and mutates the best samples in an iterative process to generate a new population of model configurations for each iteration. An important note here is that the LHS samples can be evaluated in parallel and the GA population at each iteration can be evaluated in parallel. Alternate search methods include a single Latin hypercube sample, a purely random sample, and an experimental Bayesian search method.

AUTOTUNING IN SAS MODELING PROCEDURES

The hybrid strategy for automatically tuning hyperparameters is used by a number of modeling procedures in SAS Visual Data Mining and Machine Learning. Any modeling procedure that supports autotuning provides an AUTOTUNE statement, which includes a number of options for specifically configuring what to tune and how to perform the tuning process. The following example shows how the simple addition of a single line (`autotune;`) to an existing GRADBOOST procedure script triggers the process of autotuning a gradient boosting model. The best found configuration of hyperparameters is reported as an ODS table, and the corresponding best model is saved in the specified data table (`mycaslib.mymodel`).

```
cas mysess;
libname mycaslib sasioca casref=mysess;

data mycaslib.dmagecr;
    set sampsio.dmagecr;
run;

proc gradboost data=mycaslib.dmagecr outmodel=mycaslib.mymodel;
    target good_bad / level=nominal;
    input checking duration history amount savings employed installp
        marital coapp resident property age other housing existcr job
        depends telephon foreign / level=interval;
    input purpose / level=nominal;
    autotune;
run;
```

Note: If your installation does not include the Sampsio library of examples, you will need to define it explicitly by running the following command:

```
libname sampsio '!sasroot/samples/samplesml';
```

After you run a modeling procedure that includes the AUTOTUNE statement, you will see (in addition to the standard ODS output that the procedure produces) the following additional ODS tables, which are produced by the autotuning algorithm:

- **Tuner Information** displays the tuner configuration.

- **Tuner Summary** summarizes tuner results, which include initial, best, and worst configuration; number of configurations; and tuning clock time and observed parallel speed up. (For more information, see the section "Autotuning Results and Recommendations.")

- **Tuner Task Timing** displays the time that was used for training, scoring, tuner overhead, and the overall CPU time that was required.

- **Best Configuration** provides the best configuration evaluation number, final hyperparameter values, and best configuration objective value.

- **Tuner Results** displays the initial configuration as Evaluation 0 on the first row of the table, followed by up to 10 best found configurations, sorted by their objective function value. This table enables you to compare the initial and best found configurations and potentially choose a simpler model that has nearly equivalent accuracy.

- **Tuner History** displays hyperparameter and objective values for all evaluated configurations.

Figure 7 shows some of the tables that result from running the preceding SAS script. Note that random seed generation and data distribution in SAS Viya will cause results to vary.

Tuner Information	
Model Type	Gradient Boosting Tree
Tuner Objective Function	Misclassification Error Percentage
Search Method	GA
Maximum Evaluations	50
Population Size	10
Maximum Iterations	5
Maximum Tuning Time in Seconds	36000
Validation Type	Single Partition
Validation Partition Fraction	0.3
Log Level	3
Seed	325840536

Tuner Summary	
Initial Configuration Objective Value	25.2492
Best Configuration Objective Value	22.9236
Worst Configuration Objective Value	32.8904
Initial Configuration Evaluation Time in Seconds	205.86
Best Configuration Evaluation Time in Seconds	199.53
Number of Improved Configurations	2
Number of Evaluated Configurations	45
Total Tuning Time in Seconds	1337.33
Parallel Tuning Speedup	4.7757

Tuner Task Timing		
Task	Seconds	Percent
Model Training	6294.43	98.55
Model Scoring	79.06	1.24
Total Objective Evaluations	6373.49	99.79
Tuner	13.25	0.21
Total CPU Time	6386.74	100.00

Best Configuration	
Evaluation	15
Number of Trees	121
Number of Variables to Try	18
Learning Rate	0.10852878
Sampling Rate	0.71321939
Lasso	2.36910431
Ridge	1.42146259
Misclassification Error Percentage	22.92

Tuner Results
Default and Best Configurations

Evaluation	Number of Trees	Number of Variables to Try	Learning Rate	Sampling Rate	Lasso	Ridge	Misclassification Error Percentage
0	100	20	0.100000	0.500000	0	0	25.25
15	121	18	0.108529	0.713219	2.369104	1.421463	22.92
39	120	18	0.117971	0.715619	2.518662	1.505052	23.92
10	78	18	0.450000	0.800000	7.777778	4.444444	24.25
44	122	17	0.167917	0.647899	2.607746	1.579147	24.25
37	125	18	0.101324	0.679376	2.287135	1.447222	24.58
38	124	18	0.087410	0.707852	2.034603	1.234505	24.58
14	71	20	0.088529	0.213219	0.755581	1.809792	24.92
30	122	18	0.099167	0.710840	2.220824	1.338587	24.92
1	100	20	0.100000	0.500000	0	0	25.25
6	121	9	1.000000	0.100000	4.444444	2.222222	25.25

Figure 7. SAS ODS Output Tables Produced by Autotuning

For each modeling procedure that supports autotuning, the autotuning process automatically tunes a specific subset of hyperparameters. For any hyperparameter being tuned, the procedure ignores any value that is explicitly specified in a statement other than the AUTOTUNE statement; instead the ·

autotuning process dictates both an initial value and subsequent values for candidate model configurations, either using values or ranges that are specified in the AUTOTUNE statement or using internally prescribed defaults. Table 1 lists the hyperparameters that are tuned and their corresponding defaults for the various modeling procedures.

Hyperparameter	Initial Value	Lower Bound	Upper Bound
Decision Tree (PROC TREESPLIT)			
MAXDEPTH	10	1	19
NUMBIN	20	20	200
GROW	GAIN (nominal target)	GAIN, IGR, GINI, CHISQUARE, CHAID (nominal target)	
	VARIANCE (interval target)	VARIANCE, FTEST, CHAID (interval target)	
Forest (PROC FOREST)			
NTREES	100	20	150
VARS_TO_TRY	sqrt(# inputs)	1	# inputs
INBAGFRACTION	0.6	0.1	0.9
MAXDEPTH	20	1	29
Gradient Boosting Tree (PROC GRADBOOST)			
NTREES	100	20	150
VARS_TO_TRY	# inputs	1	# inputs
LEARNINGRATE	0.1	0.01	1.0
SAMPLINGRATE	0.5	0.1	1.0
LASSO	0.0	0.0	10.0
RIDGE	0.0	0.0	10.0
Neural Network (PROC NNET)			
NHIDDEN	0	0	5
NUNITS1,...,5	1	1	100
REGL1	0	0	10.0
REGL2	0	0	10.0
LEARNINGRATE*	1 E–3	1E–6	1 E–1
ANNEALINGRATE*	1 E–6	1E–13	1 E–2
*These hyperparameters apply only when the neural net training optimization algorithm is SGD.			
Support Vector Machine (PROC SVMACHINE)			
C	1.0	1E–10	100.0
DEGREE	1	1	3
Factorization Machine (PROC FACTMAC)			
NFACTORS	5		5, 10, 15, 20, 25, 30
MAXITER	30		10, 20, 30, ..., 200
LEARNSTEP	1 E–3	1 E–6, 1 E–5, 1 E–4, 1 E–3, 1 E–2, 1 E–1, 1.0	

Table 1. Hyperparameters Driven by Autotuning in SAS Procedures

In addition to defining *what* to tune, you can set various options for *how* the tuning process should be carried out and when it should be terminated. The following example demonstrates how a few of these options can be added to the AUTOTUNE statement in the script shown earlier:

```
proc gradboost data=mycaslib.dmagecr outmodel=mycaslib.mymodel;
    target good_bad / level=nominal;
    input checking duration history amount savings employed installp
        marital coapp resident property age other housing existcr job
        depends telephon foreign / level=interval;
    input purpose / level=nominal;
    autotune popsize=5 maxiter=3 objective=ASE;
run;
```

Table 2 lists all the available AUTOTUNE options with their default values and allowed ranges. Descriptions of these options can be found in Appendix A.

Option	Default Value	Allowed Values
Optimization Algorithm Options		
MAXEVALS	50	[3–∞]
MAXITER	5	[1–∞]
MAXTIME	36,000	[1–∞]
POPSIZE	10	[2–∞]
SAMPLESIZE	50	[2–∞]
SEARCHMETHOD	GA	GA, LHS ,RANDOM, BAYESIAN
Validation Type Options		
FRACTION	0.3	[0.01–0.99]
KFOLD	5	[2–∞]
Objective Type Options		
OBJECTIVE	MSE (interval target)	MSE, ASE, RASE, MAE, RMAE, MSLE, RMSLE (interval target)
	MISC (nominal target)	MISC, ASE, RASE, MCE, MCLL, AUC, F1, F05, GINI, GAMMA, TAU (nominal target)
TARGETEVENT	First event found	
Tuning Parameters Options		
USEPARAMETERS	COMBINED	COMBINED, STANDARD, CUSTOM
TUNINGPARAMETERS	N/A	
Other Options		
EVALHISTORY	TABLE	TABLE, LOG, NONE, ALL
NPARALLEL	0	[0–∞]

Table 2. Autotuning Options

The following example shows how you can use the AUTOTUNE statement to specify several custom definitions of hyperparameters to be tuned. You can change the initial value and the range of any tuning parameter, or you can prescribe a list of specific values to be used by the autotuning process.

```
proc gradboost data=mycaslib.dmagecr outmodel=mycaslib.mymodel;
    target good_bad / level=nominal;
    input checking duration history amount savings employed installp
        marital coapp resident property age other housing existcr job
        depends telephon foreign / level=interval;
    input purpose / level=nominal;
    autotune popsize=5 maxiter=3 objective=ASE
        tuningparameters=(
            ntrees(lb=10 ub=50 init=10)
            vars_to_try(values=4 8 12 16 20 init=4)
        );
run;
```

In general, the syntax for specifying custom definitions of hyperparameters to tune is

TUNINGPARAMETERS=(*<suboption> <suboption> ...*)

where each *<suboption>* is specified as:

<hyperparameter name> (LB=*number* UB=*number* VALUES=*value-list* INIT=*number* EXCLUDE)

Descriptions of these options can be found in Appendix A.

PARALLEL EXECUTION ON THE SAS VIYA PLATFORM

Hyperparameter tuning is ideally suited for the SAS Viya distributed analytics platform. The training of a model by a machine learning algorithm can be computationally expensive. As the size of a training data set grows, not only does the expense increase, but the data (and thus the training process) must often be distributed among compute nodes because they exceed the capacity of a single computer. Also, the configurations to be considered during tuning are independent, making a sequential tuning process not only expensive but unnecessary, assuming you have an available grid of compute resources. If a cross-validation process is chosen for model validation during tuning (which is typically necessary for small data sets), the tuning process cost is multiplied by a factor of k (the number of approximately equal-sized subsets, called folds), making a sequential tuning process even more intractable and reducing the number of configurations that can be considered.

Not only are the algorithms in SAS Visual Data Mining and Machine Learning designed for distributed analysis, but the local search optimization framework is also designed to take advantage of the distributed analytics platform, allowing distributed and concurrent training and scoring of candidate model configurations. When it comes to distributed/parallel processing for hyperparameter tuning, the literature typically presents two separate modes: "data parallel" (distributed/parallel training) and "model parallel" (parallel tuning). Truly big data requires distribution of the data and the training process. The diagram in Figure 8(a) illustrates this process: multiple worker nodes are used for training and scoring each alternative model configuration, but the tuning process is a sequential loop, which might also include another inner sequential loop for the cross-validation case. Because larger data sets are more expensive to train and score, even with a distributed data and training/scoring process, this sequential tuning process can be very expensive and restrictive in the number of alternatives that can feasibly be considered in a particular period of time. The "model parallel" case is shown in Figure 8(b): multiple alternative configurations are generated and evaluated in parallel, each on a single worker node, significantly reducing the tuning time. However, the data must fit on a single worker node.

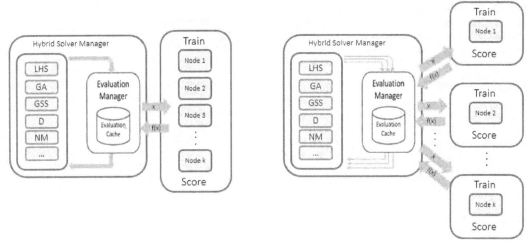

(a) "Data Parallel" (Sequential Tuning)   (b) "Model Parallel"

Figure 8. Different Uses of Distributed Computing Resources

The challenge is to determine the best usage of available worker nodes. Ideally the best usage is a combination of the "data parallel" and "model parallel" modes, finding a balance of benefit from each. Example usage of a cluster of worker nodes for model tuning presents behaviors that can guide determination of the right balance. With small problems, using multiple worker nodes for training and scoring can actually reduce performance, as shown in Figure 9(a), where a forest model is tuned for the popular **iris** data set (150 observations) for a series of different configurations. The communication cost required to coordinate distributed data and training results continually increases the tuning time—from 15 seconds on a single machine to nearly four minutes on 128 nodes. Obviously this tuning process would benefit more from parallel tuning than from distributed/parallel training.

For large data sets, benefit is observed from distributing the training process. However, the benefit of distribution and parallel processing does not continue to increase with an increasing number of worker nodes. At some point the cost of communication again outweighs the benefit of parallel processing for model training. Figure 9(b) shows that for a credit data set of 70,000 observations, the time for training and tuning increases beyond 16 nodes, to a point where 64 nodes is more costly than 1 worker node.

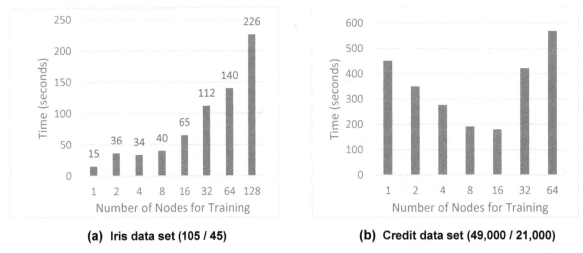

(a) Iris data set (105 / 45)   (b) Credit data set (49,000 / 21,000)

Figure 9. Distributed Training with Sequential Tuning for Different Size Data Sets (Training/Validation)

When it comes to model tuning, the "model parallel" mode (training different model configurations in parallel) typically leads to larger gains in performance, especially with small- to medium-sized data sets. The performance gain is nearly linear as the number of nodes increases because each trained model is independent during tuning—no communication is required between the different configurations being trained. The number of nodes that are used is limited based on the size of the compute grid and the search strategy (for example, the population size at each iteration of a genetic algorithm). However, it is also possible to use both "data parallel" and "model parallel" modes through careful management of the data, the training process, and the tuning process. Because managing all aspects of this process in a distributed/parallel environment is very complex, using both modes is typically not discussed in the literature or implemented in practice. However, it is implemented in the SAS Visual Data Mining and Machine Learning autotune process.

As illustrated in Figure 10(a), multiple alternate model configurations are submitted concurrently by the local search optimization framework running on the SAS Viya platform, and the individual model configurations are trained and scored on a subset of available worker nodes so that multiple nodes can be used to manage large training data and speed up the training process. Figure 10(b) shows the time reduction for tuning when this process is implemented and the number of parallel configurations is increased, with each configuration being trained on four worker nodes. The tuning time for a neural network model that is tuned to handwritten data is reduced from 11 hours to just over 1 hour when the number of parallel configurations being tuned is increased from 2 (which uses 8 worker nodes) to 32 (which uses 128 worker nodes).

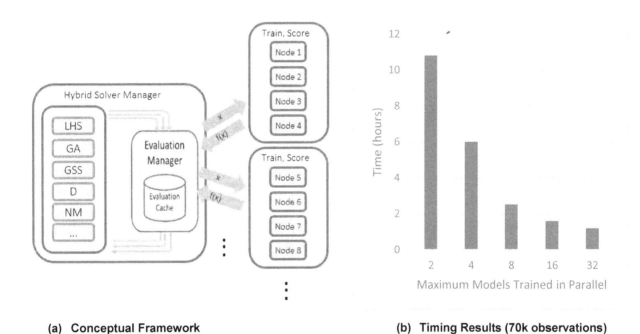

(a) **Conceptual Framework**   (b) **Timing Results (70k observations)**

Figure 10. Distributed/Parallel Training and Parallel Tuning Combined

AUTOTUNING RESULTS AND RECOMMENDATIONS

This section presents tuning results for a set of benchmark problems, showing that the tuner is behaving as expected—model error is reduced when compared to using default hyperparameter values. This section also shows tuning time results for the benchmark problems and compares validation by single partition of the data to cross-validation. Finally, a common use case is presented—the tuning of a model to recognize handwritten digits. Code samples that demonstrate the application of autotuning to these and other problems can be found at https://github.com/sassoftware/sas-viya-machine-learning/autotuning.

BENCHMARK RESULTS

Figure 11 shows model improvement (error reduction or accuracy increase—higher is better) for a suite of 10 common machine learning test problems.[1] For this benchmark study, all problems are tuned with a 30% single partition for error validation during tuning, and the conservative default autotuning process is used: five iterations with only 10 configurations per iteration in LHS and GA. All problems are run 10 times, and the results that are obtained with different validation partitions are averaged in order to better assess behavior.

Here all problems are binary classification, allowing tuning of decision trees (DT), forests (FOR), gradient boosting trees (GB), neural networks (NN), and support vector machines (SVM). Figure 11 indicates that the tuner is working—with an average reduction in model error of 2% to more than 8% across all data sets, depending on model type, when compared to a baseline model that is trained with default settings of each machine learning algorithm. You can also see a hint of the "no free lunch" theorem (Wolpert 1996) with respect to different machine learning models for different data sets; no one modeling algorithm produces the largest improvement for all problems. Some modeling algorithms show 15–20% benefit through tuning. However, note that the baseline is not shown here, only the improvement. The starting point (the initial model error) is different in each case. The largest improvement might not lead to the lowest final model error. The first problem, the **Banana** data set, suggests that NN and SVM produce the largest improvement. The **Thyroid** problem shows a very wide range of improvement for different modeling algorithms.

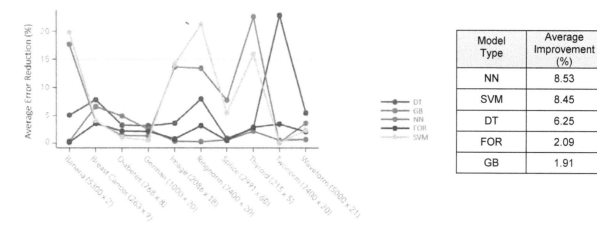

Model Type	Average Improvement (%)
NN	8.53
SVM	8.45
DT	6.25
FOR	2.09
GB	1.91

Figure 11. Benchmark Results: Average Improvement (Error Reduction) after Tuning

Figure 12 shows the final tuned model error—as averaged across the 10 tuning runs that use different validation partitions—for each problem and each modeling algorithm. The effect of the "no free lunch" theorem is quite evident here—different modeling algorithms are best for different problems. Consider the two data sets that were selected previously. For the **Banana** data set, you can see that although the improvement was best for NN and SVM, the final errors are highest for these two algorithms, indicating that the default models were worse for these modeling algorithms for this particular data set. All other modeling algorithms produce very similar error of around 10%—less than half the error from NN and SVM in this case. For the **Thyroid** data (which showed an even larger range of improvement for all modeling algorithms), the resulting model error is actually similar for different algorithms; again the default starting point is different, confirming the challenge of setting good defaults.

Overall, the benchmark results, when averaged across all data sets, are as expected. Decision trees are the simplest models and result in the highest overall average model error. If you build a forest of trees (a

---

[1] Data sets from http://mldata.org/repository/tags/data/IDA_Benchmark_Repository/, made available under the Public Domain Dedication and License v1.0, whose full text can be found at http://www.opendatacommons.org/licenses/pddl/1.0/ .

form of an ensemble model), you can reduce the error further, and for these data sets, the more complex gradient boosting training process leads to the lowest model error. The average errors for NN and SVM fall between the simple single decision tree and tree ensembles. Kernels other than linear or polynomial might be needed with SVM for these data sets, and neural networks might require more internal iterations or evaluation of more configurations, given the discrete combinations of hidden layers and units. *So why not always use gradient boosting?* Aside from fact that it might not be best for all data sets and the desire to use the simplest model that yields good predictions, there is a trade-off between resulting model accuracy and tuning time.

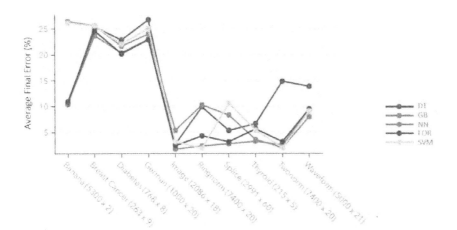

Model Type	Average Error After Tuning (%)
GB	9.9
FOR	10.7
SVM	13.1
NN	13.5
DT	13.9

Figure 12. Benchmark Results: Average Error after Tuning

TUNING TIME

For the tree-based algorithms, the trade-off is exactly the inverse ranking of machine learning algorithms with time compared to accuracy on average, as shown in Figure 13. Decision trees are the simplest and most efficient—only 14.4 seconds here for full tuning with this conservative tuning process. Building a forest of trees increases the time to over 23 seconds, and the complex gradient boosting process is more expensive at 30 seconds average tuning time. NN and SVM tuning times are similar for several problems, but higher for some, leading to a higher overall average tuning time; both use iterative optimization schemes internally to train models, and convergence might take longer for some data sets.

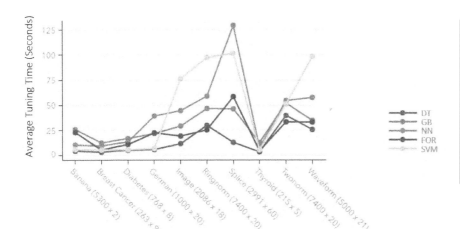

Model Type	Average Tuning Time (Seconds)	Average Parallel Speed-Up
DT	14.4	3.6
FOR	23.7	5.1
GB	30.0	4.7
NN	42.7	4.1
SVM	45.6	4.6

Figure 13. Benchmark Results: Average Total Tuning Time in Seconds

For these benchmark data sets, the tuning time is manageable—less than 30 seconds for fully tuning most models. Even the worst case, a neural network tuned to the wide **Splice** data set (which has 60 attributes) is tuned in just over two minutes. Note here again that all configurations are trained in parallel during each iteration of tuning. The total CPU time for this worst-case tuning is closer to eight minutes. With the default tuning process of 10 configurations during each of five iterations, one configuration is carried forward each iteration; so up to nine new configurations are evaluated in parallel at each iteration (by default). Figure 13 also shows parallel speed-up time (which is the total CPU time divided by the tuner clock time) of 3X–5X speed-up with parallel tuning. *Why is the speed-up not 9X with nine parallel evaluations?* Putting aside some overhead of managing parallel model training, the longest running configuration of the nine models that are trained in parallel determines the iteration time. For example, if eight configurations take 1 second each for training, and the ninth takes 2 seconds, a sequential training time of 10 seconds is reduced to 2 seconds, the longest-running model training. A 5X speed-up is observed rather than the average of the nine training times (1.1 seconds), which would be a 9X speed-up.

For larger data sets, longer-running training times, and an increased number of configurations at each iteration, the parallel speed-up will increase. For these benchmark problems, running in parallel on a compute grid might not be necessary; for a 30-second tuning time, 5X longer sequentially might not be a concern. Eight minutes for tuning the longer-running data sets might not even be a concern. Before you consider parallel/distributed training and tuning for larger data sets, however, you need to consider another tuning cost with respect to the validation process: cross-validation.

CROSS-VALIDATION

For small data sets, a single validation partition might leave insufficient data for validation in addition to training. Keeping the training and validation data representative can be a challenge. For this reason, cross-validation is typically recommended for model validation. With cross-validation, the data are partitioned into *k* approximately equal subsets called *folds*; training/scoring happens *k* times—training on all except the current holdout fold, and scoring on the holdout fold. The cross-validation error is then an average of the errors obtained from each validation fold.

This process can produce a better representation of error across the entire data set, because all observations are used for training and scoring. Figure 14 shows a comparison of cross-validation errors and the errors from a single partition, where both are compared to errors from a separate test set. The three smallest data sets are chosen, and the value in parentheses indicates the size of the holdout test set. Gradient boosting tree models are tuned in this case. The plot shows the absolute value of the error difference, where lower is better (validation error closer to test error). For the **Breast Cancer** data set, the single partition results and the cross-validation results are nearly equal. However, for the other two data sets, the cross-validation process that uses five folds produces a better representation of test error than the single validation partition does—in both cases, the cross-validation error is more than 5% closer to the test error.

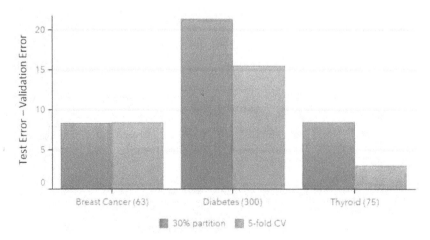

Figure 14. Benchmark Results: Single Partition versus Cross-Validation

With this cross-validation process, the trade-off is again increased time. The model training time, and therefore the overall tuning time, is increased by a factor of k. Thus, a 5X increase in time with sequential tuning for a small data set and a 5X increase with five-fold cross-validation becomes a 25X increase in tuning time. So tuning a model to even a small data set can benefit from parallel tuning.

TUNING MODELS FOR THE MNIST DIGITS DATA

In this section, the power of combined distributed modeling training and parallel tuning enabled by the SAS Viya distributed analytics platform is demonstrated by using the popular MNIST (Mixed National Institute of Standards and Technologies) database of handwritten digits (Lecun, Cortes, and Burges 2016). This database contains digitized representations of handwritten digits 0–9, in the form of a 28 × 28 image for a total of 784 pixels. Each digit image is an observation (row) in the data set, with a column for each pixel containing a grayscale value for that pixel. The database includes 60,000 observations for training, and a test set of 10,000 observations. Like many studies that use this data set, this example uses the test set for model validation during tuning.

The GRADBOOST procedure is applied to the digits database with autotuning according to the configuration that is specified in the following statements:

```
proc gradboost data=mycaslib.digits;
    partition rolevar=validvar(train='0' valid='1');
    input &inputnames;
    target label / level=nominal;
    autotune popsize=129 maxiter=20 maxevals=2560
             nparallel=32 maxtime=172800
             tuningparameters=(ntrees(ub=200));
run;
```

In this example, the training and test data sets have been combined, with the ROLEVAR= option specifying the variable that indicates which observations to use during training and which to use during scoring for validation. The PARTITION statement is used in conjunction with the AUTOTUNE statement to specify the validation approach—a single partition in this case, but using the ROLEVAR= option instead of a randomly selected percentage validation fraction. Because there are 784 potential inputs (pixels) and some of the pixels are blank for all observations, the list of input pixels that are not blank is preprocessed into the macro variable *&inputnames*, resulting in 719 inputs (see the code in Appendix B). For tuning, the number of configurations to try has been significantly increased from the default settings. Up to 20 iterations are requested, with a population size (number of configurations per iteration) of 129. Recall that one configuration is carried forward each iteration, so this specification results in up to 128 new configurations evaluated in each iteration.

A grid with 142 nodes is employed and configured to use four worker nodes per model training. *Why four instead of eight or 16 worker nodes per training as suggested in Figure 9?* There is a trade-off here for node assignment: training time versus tuning time. Using four worker nodes per training and tuning 32 models in parallel uses 128 worker nodes in total. If the number of worker nodes for training is doubled, the number of parallel models might need to be reduced in order to balance the load. Here it is decided that the gain from doubling the parallel tuning is larger than the reduced training time from doubling the number of worker nodes for each model training. Using four worker nodes, the training time for a default gradient boosting model is approximately 21.5 minutes. With eight worker nodes, the training time is approximately 13 minutes.

With up to 20 iterations and 128 configurations per iteration, the MAXEVALS= option is increased to 2,560 to accommodate these settings (the default for this option is 50, which would lead to termination before the first iteration finishes). The MAXTIME= option is also increased to support up to 48 hours of tuning time; many of the configurations train in less than the time required for the default model training.

Finally, the upper bound on the tuning range for the NTREES hyperparameter is increased to 200 from the default value of 150. The syntax enables you to override either or both of the hyperparameter bounds; in this example, the default lower bound for NTREES is unchanged and PROC GRADBOOST uses default settings for the other five tuning parameters. Increasing the upper bound for the *number of trees* hyperparameter will increase the training time for some models (and thus increase the tuning time) but might allow better models to be identified.

Some of the challenges of hyperparameter tuning discussed earlier can be seen in Figure 15, which shows the error for the configurations that are evaluated in the first iteration of tuning. Recall that the first iteration uses a Latin hypercube sample (which is more uniform than a pure random sample) to obtain an initial sample of the space. Two key points can be seen very clearly in this plot:

- The majority of the evaluated configurations produce a validation error larger than that of the default configuration, which is 2.57%.

- As you look across the plot, you can clearly see that many different configurations produce very similar error rates. These similar error rates indicate flat regions in the space, which are difficult for an optimizer to traverse and make it difficult for random configurations to identify an improved model.

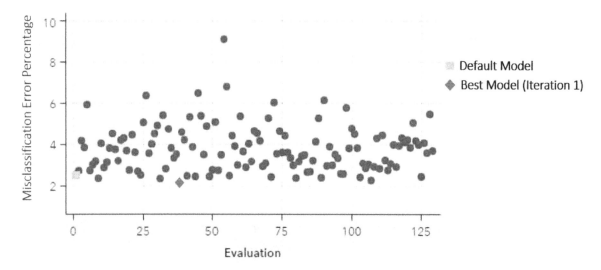

Figure 15. The GRADBOOST Procedure Tuning to MNIST Digits Data—Iteration 1

An improved model is found in the first iteration, with an error of 2.21%. Figure 16 shows the results of applying the genetic algorithm in subsequent iterations. The error is reduced again in 11 of the remaining 19 iterations. The tuning process is terminated when the maximum requested number of iterations is reached, after evaluating 2,555 unique model configurations. Here the final error is 1.74%. Details of the final model configuration are shown in Figure 17. The *number of trees* hyperparameter (which starts with a default of 100 trees) is driven up to 142 trees, still below the default upper bound of 150. Only 317 variables are used, well below the default of all (719) variables. *Learning rate* is increased from a default of 0.1 to 0.19, and *sampling rate* is increased from 0.5 to 1.0, its upper bound. Both lasso and ridge regularization begin at 0; *lasso* is increased to 0.14 and *ridge* is increased to 0.23.

Also shown in Figure 17 are tuning timing information and a tuning process summary. You can see that the tuning time of just over 28 hours (101,823 seconds) actually uses more than 760 hours of CPU time (the sum of all parallel training/scoring time for each objective evaluation), which results in a parallel speed-up of nearly 27X—much more than the 5X best case speed-up that is seen with the benchmark problems, and a much better ratio of 0.84 (with 32 parallel evaluations) compared to 0.56 (5X speed-up with 9 parallel evaluations).

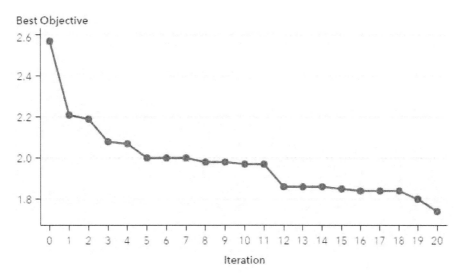

Figure 16. The GRADBOOST Procedure Tuning Iteration History, MNIST Digits Data

Best Configuration	
Evaluation	2551
Number of Trees	142
Number of Variables to Try	317
Learning Rate	0.19165378
Sampling Rate	1
Lasso	0.13883111
Ridge	0.2295815
Misclassification Error Percentage	1.74

Tuner Task Timing		
Task	Seconds	Percent
Model Training	2709131	98.98
Model Scoring	28018.86	1.02
Total Objective Evaluations	2737150	100.00
Tuner	26.84	0.00
Total CPU Time	2737177	100.00

Tuner Summary	
Initial Configuration Objective Value	2.5700
Best Configuration Objective Value	1.7400
Worst Configuration Objective Value	24.7200
Initial Configuration Evaluation Time in Seconds	1292.92
Best Configuration Evaluation Time in Seconds	1087.17
Number of Improved Configurations	18
Number of Evaluated Configurations	2555
Total Tuning Time in Seconds	101823
Parallel Tuning Speedup	26.8816

Figure 17. The GRADBOOST Procedure Tuning Results, MNIST Digits Data

CONCLUSION

The explosion of digital data is generating many opportunities for big data analytics, which in turn provides many opportunities for tuning predictive models to capitalize on the information contained in the data—to make better predictions that lead to better decisions. The tuning process often leads to hyperparameter settings that are better than the default values. But even when the default settings do work well, the hyperparameter tuning process provides a heuristic validation of these settings, giving you greater assurance that you have not overlooked a model configuration that has higher accuracy. This validation is of significant value itself.

The SAS Viya distributed analytics platform is ideally suited for tuning predictive models because many configurations often need to be evaluated. The TREESPLIT, FOREST, GRADBOOST, NNET, SVMACHINE, and FACTMAC procedures implement a fully automated tuning process that requires only the AUTOTUNE keyword to perform a conservative tuning process. This implementation includes the most commonly tuned parameters for each machine learning algorithm. You can adjust the ranges or list of values to try for these hyperparameters, exclude hyperparameters from the tuning process, and configure the tuning process itself. The local search optimization framework that is used for tuning is also ideally suited for use on the SAS Viya platform; alternate search methods can be applied and combined, with the framework managing concurrent execution and information sharing. With the complexity of the model-fitting space, many search strategies are under investigation for both effective and efficient identification of good hyperparameter values. Bayesian optimization is currently popular for hyperparameter optimization, and an experimental algorithm is available in the local search optimization framework. However, the key feature of local search optimization is its ability to build hybrid strategies that combine the strengths of *multiple* methods; no one search method will be best for tuning for all data sets and all machine learning algorithms—there is "no free lunch."

The distributed execution capability provided by the SAS Viya platform is fully exploited in this autotuning implementation. With small data sets that might not require distributed training, the need for and added expense of cross-validation support the use of parallel tuning to balance the added expense. For large data sets, distributed/parallel training and parallel model tuning can be applied concurrently within the platform for maximum benefit. One challenge is selecting the right combination of the number of worker nodes per model training and the number of parallel model configurations. With small data sets, the number of workers per training should be set as low as possible and the number of parallel configurations as high as possible, allowing the compute grid nodes to be used for parallel *tuning*. With larger data sets, such as the MNIST digits data set, a balance must be struck. Usually hundreds of worker nodes are not needed for a single model training (even with truly big data) and there is always a communication cost that can be detrimental if too many nodes are used for training. With the number of configurations evaluated in parallel, there are never "too many"—the more configurations that are evaluated in parallel, the closer to 100% efficiency the tuning process becomes, *given that many parallel configurations are not all evaluated on the same worker nodes* (evaluating hundreds of configurations on four worker nodes simultaneously will slow the process down). Approximately 84% efficiency was achieved when the PROC GRADBOOST tuning process was used to model the MNIST digits data set.

What is not discussed and demonstrated in this paper is a comparison of the implemented hybrid strategy with a random search approach for hyperparameter tuning. Random search is popular for two main reasons: a) the hyperparameter space is often discrete, which does not affect random search, and b) random search is simple and all configurations could potentially be evaluated concurrently because they are all independent. The latter reason is a strong argument when a limited number of configurations is considered or a very large grid is available. In the case of the GRADBOOST procedure tuning a model to the MNIST digits data, four nodes per training and 32 parallel configurations uses 128 nodes. The best solution was identified at evaluation 2,551. These evaluations could not have all been performed in parallel. With a combination of discrete and continuous hyperparameters, the hybrid strategy that uses a combination of Latin hypercube sampling (LHS) and a genetic algorithm (GA) is powerful; this strategy exploits the benefits of a uniform search of the space and evolves the search using knowledge gained from previous configurations. The local search optimization framework also supports random, LHS, and Bayesian search methods.

With an ever-growing collection of powerful machine learning algorithms, all governed by hyperparameters that drive their fitness quality, the "no free lunch" theorem presents yet another challenge: deciding which machine learning algorithm to tune to a particular data set. This choice is an added layer of tuning and model selection that could be managed in a model tuning framework, with parallel tuning across multiple modeling algorithms in addition to multiple configurations. Combining models of different types adds a dimension of complexity to explore with tuning. With so many variations to consider in this process, careful management of the computation process is required.

You can specify the following options in the AUTOTUNE statement:

MAXEVALS=*number* specifies the maximum number of configuration evaluations allowed for the tuner.

MAXITER=*number* specifies the maximum number of iterations of the optimization tuner.

MAXTIME=*number* specifies the maximum time (in seconds) allowed for the tuner.

POPSIZE=*number* specifies the maximum number of configurations to evaluate in one iteration (population).

SAMPLESIZE=*number* specifies the total number of configurations to evaluate when SEARCHMETHOD=RANDOM or SEARCHMETHOD=LHS.

SEARCHMETHOD=*search-method-name* specifies the search method to be used by the tuner.

FRACTION=*number* specifies the fraction of all data to be used for validation.

KFOLD=*number* specifies the number of partition folds in the cross-validation process.

EVALHISTORY=*eval-history-option* specifies the location in which to report the complete evaluation (the ODS table only, the log only, both places, or not at all).

NPARALLEL=*number* specifies the number of configurations to be evaluated by the tuner simultaneously.

OBJECTIVE=*objective-option-name* specifies the measure of model error to be used by the tuner when it searches for the best configuration.

TARGETEVENT=*target-event-name* specifies the target event to be used by the ASSESS algorithm when it calculates the error metric (used only for nominal target parameters).

USEPARAMETERS=*use-parameter-option* specifies the set of parameters to tune, with *use-parameter-option* specified as:

STANDARD tunes using the default bounds and initial values for all parameters.

CUSTOM tunes only the parameters that are specified in the TUNINGPARAMETERS= option.

COMBINED tunes the parameters that are specified in the TUNINGPARAMETERS= option and uses default bounds and initial values to tune all other parameters.

TUNINGPARAMETERS=*(suboption . . . <suboption>)* specifies the hyperparameters to tune and which ranges to tune over, with *suboption* specified as:

NAME (LB=*number* UB=*number* VALUES=*value-list* INIT=*number* EXCLUDE), where

LB specifies a custom lower bound to override the default lower bound.

UB specifies a custom upper bound to override the default upper bound.

VALUES specifies a list of values to try for this hyperparameter

INIT specifies the value to use for training a baseline model.

EXCLUDE specifies that this hyperparameter should *not* be tuned; it will remain fixed at the value specified for the procedure (or default if none is specified).

```
proc cardinality data=mycas.digits outcard=mycas.digitscard;
run;

proc sql;
  select _varname_ into :inputnames separated by ' '
    from mycas.digitscard
    where _mean_ > 0
      and _varname_ contains "pixel"
    ;
quit;
```

REFERENCES

Bergstra, J., and Bengio, Y. (2012). "Random Search for Hyper-parameter Optimization." *Journal of Machine Learning Research* 13:281–305.

Bottou, L., Curtis, F. E., and Nocedal, J. (2016). "Optimization Methods for Large-Scale Machine Learning." arXiv:1606.04838 [stat.ML].

Dewancker, I., McCourt, M., Clark, S., Hayes, P., Johnson, A., and Ke, G. (2016). "A Stratified Analysis of Bayesian Optimization Methods." arXiv:1603.09441v1 [cs.LG].

Gomes, T. A. F., Prudêncio, R. B. C., Soares, C., Rossi, A. L. D., and Carvalho, A. (2012) "Combining Meta-learning and Search Techniques to Select Parameters for Support Vector Machines." *Neurocomputing* 75:3–13.

Konen, W., Koch, P., Flasch, O., Bartz-Beielstein, T., Friese, M., and Naujoks, B. (2011). "Tuned Data Mining: A Benchmark Study on Different Tuners." In *Proceedings of the 13th Annual Conference on Genetic and Evolutionary Computation* (GECCO-2011). New York: SIGEVO/ACM.

LeCun, Y., Cortes, C., and Burges, C. J. C. (2016). "The MNIST Database of Handwritten Digits." Accessed April 8, 2016. http://yann.lecun.com/exdb/mnist/.

Lorena, A. C., and de Carvalho, A. C. P. L. F. (2008). "Evolutionary Tuning of SVM Parameter Values in Multiclass Problems." *Neurocomputing* 71:3326–3334.

McKay, M. D. (1992). "Latin Hypercube Sampling as a Tool in Uncertainty Analysis of Computer Models." In *Proceedings of the 24th Conference on Winter Simulation* (WSC 1992), edited by J. J. Swain, D. Goldsman, R. C. Crain, and J. R. Wilson, 557–564. New York: ACM.

Renukadevi, N. T., and Thangaraj, P. (2014). "Performance Analysis of Optimization Techniques for Medical Image Retrieval." *Journal of Theoretical and Applied Information Technology* 59:390–399.

Sacks, J., Welch, W. J., Mitchell, T. J., and Wynn, H. P. (1989). "Design and Analysis of Computer Experiments." *Statistical Science* 4:409–423.

Sutskever, I., Martens, J., Dahl, G., and Hinton, G. E. (2013). "On the Importance of Initialization and Momentum in Deep Learning." In *Proceedings of the 30th International Conference on Machine Learning* (ICML-13), edited by S. Dasgupta and D. McAllester, 1139–1147. International Machine Learning Society.

Wexler, J., Haller, S., and Myneni, R. 2017. "An Overview of SAS Visual Data Mining and Machine Learning on SAS Viya." In *Proceedings of the SAS Global Forum 2017 Conference*. Cary, NC: SAS Institute Inc. Available at http://support.sas.com/resources/papers/ proceedings17/SAS1492-2017.pdf.

Wolpert, D. H. (1996). "The Lack of A Priori Distinctions between Learning Algorithms." *Neural Computation* 8:1341–1390.

Wujek, B., Hall, P., and Güneş, F. (2016). "Best Practices in Machine Learning Applications." In *Proceedings of the SAS Global Forum 2016 Conference*. Cary, NC: SAS Institute Inc. https://support.sas.com/resources/papers/proceedings16/SAS2360-2016.pdf.

ACKNOWLEDGMENTS

The authors would like to thank Joshua Griffin, Scott Pope, and Anne Baxter for their contributions to this paper.

RECOMMENDED READING

- *Getting Started with SAS Visual Data Mining and Machine Learning 8.1*
- *SAS Visual Data Mining and Machine Learning 8.1: Data Mining and Machine Learning Procedures*
- *SAS Visual Data Mining and Machine Learning 8.1: Statistical Procedures*

CONTACT INFORMATION

Your comments and questions are valued and encouraged. Contact the authors:

Patrick Koch
SAS Institute Inc.
patrick.koch@sas.com

Brett Wujek
SAS Institute Inc.
brett.wujek@sas.com

Oleg Golovidov
SAS Institute Inc.
oleg.golovidov@sas.com

Steven Gardner
SAS Institute Inc.
steven.gardner@sas.com

Stacked Ensemble Models for Improved Prediction Accuracy

Funda Güneş, Russ Wolfinger, and Pei-Yi Tan

SAS Institute Inc.

ABSTRACT

Ensemble modeling is now a well-established means for improving prediction accuracy; it enables you to average out noise from diverse models and thereby enhance the generalizable signal. Basic stacked ensemble techniques combine predictions from multiple machine learning algorithms and use these predictions as inputs to second-level learning models. This paper shows how you can generate a diverse set of models by various methods such as forest, gradient boosted decision trees, factorization machines, and logistic regression and then combine them with stacked-ensemble techniques such as hill climbing, gradient boosting, and nonnegative least squares in SAS® Visual Data Mining and Machine Learning. The application of these techniques to real-world big data problems demonstrates how using stacked ensembles produces greater prediction accuracy and robustness than do individual models. The approach is powerful and compelling enough to alter your initial data mining mindset from finding the single best model to finding a collection of really good complementary models. It does involve additional cost due both to training a large number of models and the proper use of cross validation to avoid overfitting. This paper shows how to efficiently handle this computational expense in a modern SAS® environment and how to manage an ensemble workflow by using parallel computation in a distributed framework.

INTRODUCTION

Ensemble methods are commonly used to boost predictive accuracy by combining the predictions of multiple machine learning models. Model stacking is an efficient ensemble method in which the predictions that are generated by using different learning algorithms are used as inputs in a second-level learning algorithm. This second-level algorithm is trained to optimally combine the model predictions to form a final set of predictions (Sill et al. 2009).

In the last decade, model stacking has been successfully used on a wide variety of predictive modeling problems to boost the models' prediction accuracy beyond the level obtained by any of the individual models. This is sometimes referred to as a "wisdom of crowds" approach, pulling from the age-old philosophy of Aristotle. Ensemble modeling and model stacking are especially popular in data science competitions, in which a sponsor posts training and test data and issues a global challenge to produce the best model for a specified performance criterion. The winning model is almost always an ensemble model. Often individual teams develop their own ensemble model in the early stages of the competition and then join forces in the later stages. One such popular site is Kaggle, and you are encouraged to explore numerous winning solutions that are posted in the discussion forums there to get a flavor of the state of the art.

The diversity of the models in a library plays a key role in building a powerful ensemble model. Dietterich (2000) emphasizes the importance of diversity by stating, "A necessary and sufficient condition for an ensemble model to be more accurate than any of its individual members is if the classifiers are accurate and diverse." By combining information from diverse modeling approaches, ensemble models gain more accuracy and robustness than a fine-tuned single model can gain. There are many parallels with successful human teams in business, science, politics, and sports, in which each team member makes a significant contribution and individual weaknesses and biases are offset by the strengths of other members.

Overfitting is an omnipresent concern in ensemble modeling because a model library includes so many models that predict the same target. As the number of models in a model library increases, the chances of building overfitting ensemble models increases greatly. A related problem is leakage, in which

1

information from the target inadvertently and sometimes surreptitiously works its way into the model-checking mechanism and causes an overly optimistic assessment of generalization performance. The most efficient techniques that practitioners commonly use to minimize overfitting and leakage include cross validation, regularization, and bagging. This paper covers applications of these techniques for building ensemble models that can generalize well to new data.

This paper first provides an introduction to SAS Visual Data Mining and Machine Learning in SAS® Viya™, which is a new single, integrated, in-memory environment. The section following that discusses how to generate a diverse library of machine learning models for stacking while avoiding overfitting and leakage, and then shows an approach to building a diverse model library for a binary classification problem. A subsequent section shows how to perform model stacking by using regularized regression models, including nonnegative least squares regression. Another section demonstrates stacking with the scalable gradient boosting algorithm and focuses on an automatic tuning implementation that is based on efficient distributed and parallel paradigms for training and tuning models in the SAS Viya platform. The penultimate section shows how to build powerful ensemble models with the hill climbing technique. The last section compares the stacked ensemble models that are built by each approach to a naïve ensemble model and the single best model, and also provides a brief summary.

OVERVIEW OF THE SAS VIYA ENVIRONMENT

The SAS programs used in this paper are built in the new SAS Viya environment. SAS Viya uses SAS® Cloud Analytic Services (CAS) to perform tasks and enables you to build various model scenarios in a consistent environment, resulting in improved productivity, stability, and maintainability. SAS Viya represents a major rearchitecture of core data processing and analytical components in SAS software to enable computations across a large distributed grid in which it is typically more efficient to move algorithmic code rather than to move data.

The smallest unit of work for the CAS server is a CAS action. CAS actions can load data, transform data, compute statistics, perform analytics, and create output. Each action is configured by specifying a set of input parameters. Running a CAS action in the CAS server processes the action's parameters and the data to create an action result.

In SAS Viya, you can run CAS actions via a variety of interfaces, including the following:

- SAS session, which uses the CAS procedure. PROC CAS uses the CAS language (CASL) for specifying CAS actions and their input parameters. The CAS language also supports normal program logic such as conditional and looping statements and user-written functions.

- Python or Lua, which use the SAS Scripting Wrapper for Analytics Transfer (SWAT) libraries

- Java, which uses the CAS Client class

- Representational state transfer (REST), which uses the CAS REST APIs

CAS actions are organized into action sets, where each action set defines an application programming interface (API). SAS Viya currently provides the following action sets:

- Data mining and machine learning action sets support gradient boosted trees, neural networks, factorization machines, support vector machines, graph and network analysis, text mining, and more.

- Statistics action sets compute summary statistics and perform clustering, regression, sampling, principal component analysis, and more.

- Analytics action sets provide additional numeric and text analytics.

- System action sets run SAS code via the DATA step or DS2, manage CAS libraries and tables, manage CAS servers and sessions, and more.

SAS Viya also provides CAS-powered procedures, which enable you to have the familiar experience of coding traditional SAS procedures. Behind each statement in these procedures is one or more CAS actions that run across multiple machines. The SAS Viya platform enables you to program with both CAS actions and procedures, providing you with maximum flexibility to build an optimal ensemble.

SAS Visual Data Mining and Machine Learning integrates CAS actions and CAS-powered procedures and surfaces in-memory machine-learning techniques such as gradient boosting, factorization machines, neural networks, and much more through its interactive visual interface, SAS® Studio tasks, procedures, and a Python client. This product bundle is an industry-leading platform for analyzing complex data, building predictive models, and conducting advanced statistical operations (Wexler, Haller, and Myneni 2017).

For more information about SAS Viya and SAS Visual Data Mining and Machine Learning, see the section "Recommended Reading." For specific code examples from this paper, refer to the Github repository referenced in that section.

BUILDING A STRONG LIBRARY OF DIVERSE MODELS

You can generate a diverse set of models by using many different machine learning algorithms at various hyperparameter settings. Forest and gradient bosting methods are themselves based on the idea of combining diverse decision tree models. The forest method generates diverse models by training decision trees on a number of bootstrap samples of the training set, whereas the gradient boosting method generates a diverse set of models by fitting models to sequentially adjusted residuals, a form of stochastic gradient descent. In a broad sense, even multiple regression models can be considered to be an ensemble of single regression models, with weights determined by least squares. Whereas the traditional wisdom in the literature is to combine so-called "weak" learners, the modern approach is to create an ensemble of a well-chosen collection of strong yet diverse models.

In addition to using many different modeling algorithms, the diversity in a model library can be further enhanced by randomly subsetting the rows (observations) and/or columns (features) in the training set. Subsetting rows can be done with replacement (bootstrap) or without replacement (for example, k-fold cross validation). The word "bagging" is often used loosely to describe such subsetting; it can also be used to describe subsetting of columns. Columns can be subsetted randomly or in a more principled fashion that is based on some computed measure of importance. The variety of choices for subsetting columns opens the door to the large and difficult problem of feature selection.

Each new big data set tends to bring its own challenges and intricacies, and no single fixed machine learning algorithm is known to dominate. Furthermore, each of the main classes of algorithms has a set of hyperparameters that must be specified, leading to an effectively infinite set of possible models you can fit. In order to navigate through this model space and achieve near optimal performance for a machine learning task, a basic brute-force strategy is to first build a reasonably large collection of model fits across a well-designed grid of settings and then compare, reduce, and combine them in some intelligent fashion. A modern distributed computing framework such as SAS Viya makes this strategy quite feasible.

AVOIDING LEAKAGE WHILE STACKING

A naïve ensembling approach is to directly take the predictions of the test data from a set of models that are fit on the full training set and use them as inputs to a second-level model, say a simple regression model. This approach is almost guaranteed to overfit the data because the target responses have been used twice, a form of data leakage. The resulting model almost always generalizes poorly for a new data set that has previously unseen targets. The following subsections describe the most common techniques for combatting leakage and selecting ensembles that will perform well on future data.

SINGLE HOLDOUT VALIDATION SET

The classic way to avoid overfitting is to set aside a fraction of the training data and treat its target labels as unseen until final evaluation of a model fitting process. This approach has been the main one available in SAS Enterprise Miner from its inception, and it remains a simple and reliable way to assess model accuracy. It can be the most efficient way to compare models. It also is the way most data science competitions are structured for data sets that have a large number of rows.

For stacked ensembling, this approach also provides a good way to assess ensembles that are made on the dedicated training data. However, it provides no direct help in constructing those ensembles, nor does it provide any measure of variability in the model performance metric because you obtain only a single number. The latter concern can be addressed by scoring a set of bootstrap or other well-chosen random samples of the single holdout set.

K-FOLD CROSS VALIDATION AND OUT-OF-FOLD PREDICTIONS

The main idea of cross validation is to repeat the single holdout concept across different folds of the data—that is, to sequentially train a model on one part of the data and then observe the behavior of this trained model on the other held-out part, for which you know the ground truth. Doing so enables you to simulate performance on previously unseen targets and aims to decrease the bias of the learners with respect to the training data.

Assuming that each observation has equal weight, it makes sense to hold out each with equal frequency. The original jackknife (leave-one-out cross validation) method in regression holds out one observation at a time, but this method tends to be computationally infeasible for more complex algorithms and large data sets. A better approach is to hold out a significant fraction of the data (typically 10 or 20%) and divide the training data into k folds, where k is 5 or 10. The following simple steps are used to obtain five-fold cross validated predictions:

1. Divide the training data into five disjoint folds of as nearly equal size as possible, and possibly also stratify by target frequencies or means.
2. Hold out each fold one at a time.
3. Train the model on the remaining data.
4. Assess the trained model by using the holdout set.

Fitting and scoring for all k versions of the training and holdout sets provides holdout (cross validated) predictions for each of the samples in your original training data. These are known as out-of-fold (OOF) predictions. The sum of squared errors between the OOF predictions and true target values yields the cross validation error of a model, and is typically a good measure of generalizability. Furthermore, the OOF predictions are usually safely used as inputs for second-level stacked ensembling.

You might be able to further increase the robustness of your OOF predictions by repeating the entire k-fold exercise, recomputing OOFs with different random folds, and averaging the results. However, you must be careful to avoid possible subtle leakage if too many repetitions are done. Determining the best number of repetitions is not trivial. You can determine the best number by doing nested k-fold cross validation, in which you perform two-levels of k-fold cross validation (one within the other) and assess performance at the outer level. In this nested framework, the idea is to evaluate a small grid of repetition numbers, determine which one performs best, and then use this number for subsequent regular k-fold evaluations. You can also use this approach to help choose k if you suspect that the common values of 5 or 10 are suboptimal for your data.

Cross validation can be used both for tuning hyperparameters and for evaluating model performance. When you use the same data both for tuning and for estimating the generalization error with k-fold cross validation, you might have information leakage and the resulting model might overfit the data. To deal with this overfitting problem, you can use nested k-fold cross validation—you use the inner loop for parameter tuning, and you use the outer loop to estimate the generalization error (Cawley and Talbot 2010).

BAGGING AND OUT-OF-BAG PREDICTIONS

A technique similar in spirit to k-fold cross-validation is classical bagging, in which numerous bootstrap samples (with replacement) are constructed and the out-of-bag (OOB) predictions are used to assess model performance. One potential downside to this approach is the uneven number of times each observation is held out and the potential for some missing values. However, this downside is usually inconsequential if you perform an appropriate number of bootstrap repetitions (for example, 100). This type of operation is very suitable for parallel processing, where with the right framework generating 100 bootstrap samples will not take much more clock time than 10 seconds.

EXAMPLE: ADULT SALARY DATA SET

This section describes how to build a strong and diverse model library by using the Adult data set from the UCI Machine Learning Repository (Lichman 2013). This data set has 32,561 training samples and16,281 test samples; it includes 13 input variables, which are a mix of nominal and interval variables that include education, race, marital status, capital gain, and capital loss. The target is a binary variable that takes a value of 1 if a person makes less than 50,000 a year and value of 0 otherwise. The training and test set are available in a GitHub repository, for which a link is provided in the section "Recommended Reading."

Treating Nominal Variables

The data set includes six nominal variables that have various levels. The cardinality of the categorical variables is reduced by collapsing the rare categories and making sure that each distinct level has at least 2% of the samples. For example, the cardinality of the work class variable is reduced from 8 to 7, and the cardinality of the occupation variable is reduced from 14 to 12.

The nominal variable *education* is dropped from the analysis, because the corresponding interval variable (*education_num*) already exists. All the remaining nominal variables are converted to numerical variables by using likelihood encoding as described in the next section.

Likelihood Encoding and Feature Engineering

Likelihood encoding involves judiciously using the target variable to create numeric versions of categorical features. The most common way of doing this is to replace each level of the categorical variable with the mean of the target over all observations that have that level. Doing this carries a danger of information leakage that might result in significant overfitting. The best way to combat the danger of leakage is to perform the encoding separately for each distinct version of the training data during cross validation. For example, while doing five-fold cross validation, you compute the likelihood-encoded categorical variable anew for each of the five training sets and use these values in the corresponding holdout sets. A drawback of this approach is the extra calculations and bookkeeping that are required.

If the cardinality of a categorical variable is small relative to the number of observations and if the binary target is not rare, it can be acceptable to do the likelihood encoding once up front and run the risk of a small amount of leakage. For the sake of illustration and convenience, that approach is taken here with the Adult data set, because the maximum cardinality of the nominal variables is 12.

Likelihood encoding has direct ties to classical statistical methods such as one-way ANOVA, and it can be viewed as stacking the simple predictions from such models. More sophisticated versions involve shrinking the encoded means toward an overall mean, which can be particularly effective when the class sizes are imbalanced. This approach is well-known to improve mean square prediction error and is popularly known as L2 regularization in machine learning communities and as ridge regression or best linear unbiased prediction (BLUP) in statistical communities. Alternatively, you can use an L1 (LASSO) norm and shrink toward the median. Note also that likelihood encoding effectively performs the same operation that tree-based methods perform at their first step—that is, sorting categories by their target likelihood in order to find the best way to split them into two groups.

Stacking and Building the Model Library

As an illustrative small example, you can use the following three-level stacked ensemble approach along with four different machine learning algorithms (gradient boosting, forest, factorization machines, and logistic regression):

Level 1: Fit initial models and find good hyperparameters using cross validation and automatic tuning (also called autotuning).

Level 2: Create 100 bootstrap samples of the training set, and subsequently divide each of these samples into five folds. For each individual training set, train the four models (by using five-fold cross validation) and create 100 sets of five-fold OOF predictions. This approach effectively creates 400 total OOF predictions with approximately 1/3 of the values missing because of the properties of bootstrap (with replacement) sampling.

Level 3: Average together the nonmissing OOF predictions for each learning algorithm, creating four total average OOF predictions (one for each learning algorithm). Use LASSO, nonnegative least squares, gradient boosting, and hill climbing on these four features to obtain the final predictions.

As you move through the levels, you also create features on the final testing data. It is usually wise to keep training and testing features close to each other while coding. Otherwise you increase the risk of making a mistake at testing time because of an oversight in indexing or scoring. This practice also helps you keep your final goal in mind and ensure that everything you are doing is applicable to unlabeled testing rows.

Results for Level 1

Level 1 creates an initial small diverse library of models by using gradient boosting, forest, factorization machines, and logistic regression on the SAS Viya platform, which trains and tunes models quickly via in-memory processing by taking advantage of both multithreading and distributed computing. These algorithms include a fair number of hyperparameters that must be specified, and a manual tuning process can be difficult. Instead, you can use the efficient random search capability in the AUTOTUNE statement available in the GRADBOOST (scalable gradient boosting), FOREST, and the FACTMAC (factorization machines) procedures. By using autotuning, you can rapidly reduce the model error that is produced by default settings of these hyperparameters. This automated search provides an efficient search path through the hyperparameter space by taking advantage of parallel computing in the SAS Viya platform. The AUTOTUNE statement is also available in the NNET (neural network), TREESPLIT (decision tree), and SVMACHINE (support vector machine) procedures of SAS Viya Data Mining and Machine Learning. You can see an example of how autotuning is used in the section "Stacking with the Scalable Gradient Boosting Algorithm." You must be wary of overfitting and leakage while doing this tuning. For more information about automated search, see Koch et al. (2017).

Results for Level 2

After finding good set of hyperparameter values for each of the four modeling algorithms, Level 2 generates 100 bootstrap replications (sampling with replacement) of the training data. Each training set is then divided into five disjoint folds, which produces five versions of new training sets (each version omits one fold) for each of the bootstrap samples. Notice that this setup produces 500 (100 x 5) versions of training sets. Forest, gradient boosting, factorization machine, and logistic regression models are trained on each of these training sets and the left-out folds are scored. In total, 2,000 (500 x 4) models are trained and scored. For each bootstrap sample, the five sets of OOF predictions are combined, which produces 400 columns of five-fold OOF predictions (100 gradient boosting, 100 forest, 100 logistic models, and 100 factorization machines).

Because bootstrap sampling uses sampling with replacement, it results in some missing predictions in addition to multiple predictions for the same IDs. This example adopts the following approach to deal with these issues and arrive at one prediction for each ID:

- If an ID is selected more than once, the average prediction is used for each ID.

- After making sure that each ID is selected at least once in the 100 bootstrap samples of each modeling algorithm, mean OOF predictions are obtained by averaging over 100 bootstrap OOF predictions. This simple averaging provided a significant reduction in the five-fold training ASE. For example, for the gradient boosting model, the five-fold training ASE of the best model (out of 100 models) was 0.09351. When the OOF predictions of 100 gradient boosting models are averaged, this value reduced to 0.09236.

This approach produces four columns of OOF predictions (one for each of the four algorithms). These four averaged models form the model library to be used in Level-3 stacking.

For scoring on test data, the predictions from the 500 models, which are generated by the same learning algorithm, are simply averaged.

Figure 1 shows the five-fold cross validation and test average squared errors (ASEs, also often called mean squared error, or MSE) of the four average models that form the model library to be used in Level-3 stacking. The best performing single modeling method is the average gradient boosting model, which has a five-fold cross validation ASE of 0.09236. It is best by a fairly significant margin according to the ASE performance metric.

Level-2 Models	Training ASE (Five-Fold CV ASE)	Testing ASE
Average gradient boosting	0.09236	0.09273
Average forest	0.09662	0.09665
Average logistic regression	0.10470	0.10370
Average factorization machines	0.11160	0.10930

Figure 1. Five-Fold Cross Validation and Test ASEs of Models in the Model Library

Results for Level 3

With average OOF predictions in hand from Level 2, you are ready to build final ensembles and assess the resulting models by using the test set predictions. The OOF predictions are stored in the SAS data set train_mean_oofs, which includes four columns of OOF predictions for the four average models, an ID variable, and the target variable. The corresponding test set is test_mean_preds which includes the same columns. The rest of the analyses in this paper use these two data sets, which are also available in the GitHub repository.

Start a CAS Session and Load Data into CAS

The following SAS code starts a CAS session and loads data into in the CAS in-memory distributed computing engine in the SAS Viya environment:

```
/* Start a CAS session named mySession */
cas mySession;

/* Define a CAS engine libref for CAS in-memory data tables  */
/* Define a SAS libref for the directory that includes the data */
libname cas sasioca;
libname data "/folders/myfolders/";

/* Load data into CAS using SAS DATA steps */
data cas.train_oofs;
   set data.train_mean_oofs;
run;
data cas.test_preds;
   set data.test_mean_preds;
run;
```

Let Y represent the target, X represent the space of inputs, and $g_1, ..., g_L$ denote the learned predictions from L machine learning algorithms (for example, a set of out-of-fold predictions). For an interval target, a linear ensemble model builds a prediction function,

$$b(g) = w_1 * g_1 + \cdots + w_L * g_L$$

where w_i are the model weights. A simple way to specify these weights is to set them all equal to $1/L$ (as done in Level-2) so that each model contributes equally to the final ensemble. You can alternatively assign higher weight to models you think will perform better. For the Adult example, the gradient boosted tree OOF predictor is a natural candidate to weight higher because of its best single model performance.

Although assigning weights by hand can often be reasonable, you can typically improve final ensemble performance by using a learning algorithm to estimate them. Because of its computational efficiency and model interpretability, linear regression is a commonly used method for final model stacking. In a regression model that has an interval target, the model weights (w_i) are found by solving the following least squares problem:

$$min \sum_{i=1}^{N} (y_i - (w_1 * g_{1i} + \cdots + w_L * g_{Li}))^2$$

REGULARIZATION

Using cross validated predictions partially helps to deal with the overfitting problem. An attending difficulty with using OOF or OOB predictions as inputs is that they tend to be highly correlated with each other, creating the well-known collinearity problem for regression fitting. Arguably the best way to deal with this problem is to use some form of regularization for the model weights when training the highest-level model. Regularization methods place one or more penalties on the objective function, based on the size of the model weights. If these penalty parameters are selected correctly, the total prediction error of the model can decrease significantly and the parameters of the resulting model can be more stable.

The following subsections illustrate a couple of good ways to regularize your ensemble model. They involve estimating and choosing one or more new hyperparameters that control the amount of regularization. These hyperparameters can be determined by various methods, including a single validation data partition, cross validation, and information criteria.

Stacking with Adaptive LASSO

Consider a linear regression of the following form:

$$b(x) = w_1 * g_1 + \cdots + w_L * g_L$$

A LASSO learner finds the model weights by placing an L_1 (sum of the absolute value of the weights) penalty on the model weights as follows:

$$min \sum_{i=1}^{N} (y_i - (w_1 * g_{1i} + \cdots + w_L * g_{Li}))^2$$

$$\text{subject to} \sum_{i=1}^{L} |w_i| \leq t$$

If the LASSO hyperparameter t is small enough, some of the weights will be exactly 0. Thus, the LASSO method produces a sparser and potentially more interpretable model. Adaptive LASSO (Zou 2006) modifies the LASSO penalty by applying adaptive weights (v_j) to each parameter that forms the LASSO constraint:

$$\text{subject to } \sum_{i=1}^{L} (v_i |w_i|) \leq t$$

These constraints control shrinking the zero coefficients more than they control shrinking the nonzero coefficients.

The following REGSELECT procedure run builds an adaptive LASSO model. By default, the procedure uses the inverse of the full linear regression model coefficients for v_j (Güneş 2015).

```
proc regselect data=cas.train_mean_oofs;
    partition fraction(validate=0.3);
    model target = mean_factmac mean_gbt mean_logit mean_frst / noint;
    selection method=lasso
        (adaptive stop=sbc choose=validate) details=steps;
    code file="/c/output/lasso_score.sas";
run;
```

The PARTITION statement reserves 30% of the data for validation, leaving the remaining 70% for training. The validation part of the data is used to find the optimal value for the adaptive LASSO parameter t. The MODEL statement specifies the four average OOF predictions from Level 2 as input variables. The SELECTION statement requests the adaptive LASSO method, and the CHOOSE=VALIDATE suboption requests that the selected regularization parameter (t) be used to minimize the validation error on the 30% single holdout set. The CODE statement saves the resulting scoring code in the specified directory.

Figure 2 shows the results. The gradient boosted predictor receives around 94% of the weight in the resulting ensemble, with the remaining 6% going to the forest model, along with just a little contribution from factorization machines. The ASE appears to have improved a little, but keep in mind that these results are on a new 30% holdout.

Parameter Estimates		
Parameter	DF	Estimate
mean_factmac	1	0.001931
mean_gbt	1	0.938671
mean_frst	1	0.058570

ASE (Train)	0.09214
ASE (Validate)	0.09263

Figure 2. Parameter Estimates and Fit statistics for the Adaptive LASSO Stacking Model

To obtain a better measure of prediction error, you can check the ASE of the resulting model for the test set. The following SAS statements first score for the test set by using the saved score code, lasso_score.sas, and then calculate the ASE:

9

```
data cas.lasso_score;
    set cas.test_preds;
    %include '/c/output/lasso_score.sas';
run;

data cas.lasso_score;
    se=(p_target-target)*(p_target-target);
run;

proc cas;
    summary/ table={name='lasso_score', vars={'se'}};
run;
quit;
```

The **summary** CAS action outputs the test ASE of the adaptive LASSO ensemble model as 0.09269, which improves slightly on the average gradient boosting model, whose test ASE is 0.09273.

Stacking with Nonnegative Weights Regularization

Another regularization technique that is commonly used to build a stacked regression model is to restrict the regression coefficients to be nonnegative while performing regression. Breiman (1995) shows that when the regression coefficients are constrained to be nonnegative, the resulting ensemble models exhibit better prediction error than any of the individual models in the library. Because each model takes a nonnegative weight, the resulting ensemble model can also be interpreted more easily. The paper also shows that the additional commonly used restriction $\Sigma\, w_i = 1$ does not further improve the prediction accuracy, which is consistent with the findings here for the Adult data. A linear regression model that places nonnegative weights on a squared error loss function has the following form:

$$\min \sum_{i=1}^{N} (y_i - (w_1 * g_{1i} + \cdots + w_L * g_{Li}))^2$$

$$\text{subject to } w_i > 0, \qquad \text{for } i = 1, \dots, L$$

The following CQLIM procedure statements from SAS® Econometrics fit a linear least squares regression model with nonnegativity constraints on the regression weights:

```
proc cqlim data=cas.train_mean_oofs;
    model target= mean_gbt mean_frst mean_logit mean_factmac;
    restrict mean_gbt>0;
    restrict mean_frst>0;
    restrict mean_logit>0;
    restrict mean_factmac>0;
    output out=cas.cqlim_preds xbeta copyvar=target;
    ods output ParameterEstimates=paramests;
run;
```

Figure 3 shows the "Parameter Estimates" table that is generated by the CQLIM procedure. The Estimate column shows the regression weights of the stacked nonnegative least squares model for each of the four models. Here factorization machines have a slightly larger weight than in the previous adaptive LASSO model.

10

Parameter Estimates					
Parameter	DF	Estimate	Standard Error	t Value	Approx Pr > |t|
mean_gbt	1	0.921430	0.024091	38.25	<.0001
mean_factmac	1	0.022345	0.012701	1.76	0.0785
mean_frst	1	0.056071	0.025714	2.18	0.0292
mean_logit	1	1.0536712E-8	0	.	

Figure 3. Regression Weights for the Nonnegative Least Squares Stacking Model

This stacked model produces a training error of 0.09228 and a testing error of 0.09269, which provides an improvement over the single best Level-2 model: the average gradient boosting model, which has a training ASE of 0.09236 and a testing ASE of 0.09273.

STACKING WITH THE SCALABLE GRADIENT BOOSTING ALGORITHM AND AUTOTUNING

Model stacking is not limited to basic models such as linear regression; any supervised learning algorithm can be used as a higher-level learning algorithm as long as it helps boost the prediction accuracy. In fact, nonlinear algorithms such as boosted trees and neural networks have been successfully used as a second- and third-level modeling algorithms in winning methods of various data science competitions.

The GRADBOOST procedure in SAS Visual Data Mining and Machine Learning fits a scalable gradient boosting model that is based that is on the boosting method described in Hastie, Tibshirani, and Friedman (2001), and its functionality is comparable to the popular **xgboost** program. PROC GRADBOOST is computationally efficient and uses fewer resources than the Gradient Boosting node in SAS Enterprise Miner uses.

The following GRADBOOST procedure run trains a stacked ensemble model by using the Level-2 OOF predictions of the four average models:

```
proc gradboost data=cas.train_mean_oofs outmodel=cas.gbt_ensemble;
    target target / level=nominal;
    input mean_factmac mean_gbt mean_logit mean_frst / level=interval;
    autotune tuningparameters=(ntrees samplingrate vars_to_try(init=4)
            learningrate(ub=0.3) lasso ridge) searchmethod=random
            samplesize=200 objective=ase kfold=5;
    ods output FitStatistics=Work._Gradboost_FitStats_
            VariableImportance=Work._Gradboost_VarImp_;
run;
```

The OUTMODEL option in the PROC statement saves the resulting trained model as a CAS table called gbt_ensemble. This table is used later for scoring the test data. The TARGET statement specifies the binary target variable, and the INPUT statement specifies the average OOF predictions that are obtained from Level-2 average models for gradient boosting, forest, logistic regression, and factorization machines.

The AUTOTUNE statement performs an automatic search for the optimal hyperparameter settings of the gradient boosting algorithm. It specifies a random search among 200 randomly selected hyperparameter settings of the gradient boosting algorithm. For assessing the resulting models, five-fold cross validation is used with the ASE metric that is specified by the following suboptions of the AUTOTUNE statement: OBJECTIVE=ASE KFOLD=5. The AUTOTUNE statement performs a search for the following parameters of the gradient boosting algorithm: number of iterations, sampling proportion, number of variables to try, learning rate, and LASSO and ridge regularization parameters. For other parameters, the procedure uses default values (the maximum depth of a tree is 5, the maximum number of observations for a leaf is 5, and the maximum number of branches for a node is 2), but these values can also be optionally tuned. To further control the parameter search process, you can specify upper bounds, lower bounds, and initial values for the hyperparameters. The preceding statements specify an upper bound for the learning rate parameter, LEARNINGRATE (UB=0.2), and an initial value for the number of variables to try, VARS_TO_TRY (INIT=4).

Figure 4 summarizes the autotuning options that are specified in the AUTOTUNE statement.

Tuner Information	
Model Type	Gradient Boosting Tree
Tuner Objective Function	Average Squared Error
Search Method	RANDOM
Maximum Evaluations	201
Sample Size	200
Maximum Tuning Time in Seconds	36000
Validation Type	Cross-Validation
Num Folds in Cross-Validation	5
Log Level	2
Seed	1669463436

Figure 4. Autotuning Information Table

Figure 5 shows the resulting best configuration hyperparameter values.

Best Configuration	
Evaluation	86
Number of Trees	56
Number of Variables to Try	3
Learning Rate	0.10990335
Sampling Rate	0.75938235
Lasso	3.25403452
Ridge	3.64367127
Average Squared Error	0.09

Figure 5. Autotuning Best Hyperparameter Settings for the Stacking Gradient Boosting Model

The "Tuner Summary" table in Figure 6 shows that the five-fold ASE for the best configuration of hyperparameter values is 0.09245.

Tuner Summary	
Initial Configuration Objective Value	0.09330
Best Configuration Objective Value	0.09245
Worst Configuration Objective Value	0.1448
Initial Configuration Evaluation Time in Seconds	10.4112
Best Configuration Evaluation Time in Seconds	9.2367
Number of Improved Configurations	5
Number of Evaluated Configurations	201
Total Tuning Time in Seconds	300.98
Parallel Tuning Speedup	10.1676

Figure 6. Autotuning Summary Table for the Stacking Gradient Boosting Model

Figure 6 also reports the total tuning time to be 5 minutes. This time is based on using 100 nodes in a SAS Viya distributed analytics platform. Note that five-fold cross validation is used as an assessment measure and models are assessed for 200 different hyperparameter settings, which requires fitting and scoring for 1,000 models. Each training set includes approximately 25,600 samples (4/5 of the full training set) and 4 features, and training and scoring for one model took around 0.35 seconds. This brief amount of time is made possible by taking full advantage of in-memory parallel computing not only for running each gradient boosting model but also for performing a random search for hyperparameter tuning.

The output also includes a table of the parameter settings and the corresponding five-fold ASEs for all 200 hyperparameter settings. Figure 7 shows the best 10 models that are found by the autotuning functionality. The AUTOTUNE statement in SAS Viya machine learning procedures has even more extensive capabilities that are not covered here; for more information and full capabilities, see Koch et al. (2017).

Tuner Results Default and Best Configurations							
Evaluation	Number of Trees	Number of Variables to Try	Learning Rate	Sampling Rate	Lasso	Ridge	Average Squared Error
0	100	4	0.100000	0.500000	0	0	0.0933
86	56	3	0.109903	0.759382	3.254035	3.643671	0.0924
78	84	3	0.078068	0.618316	7.852888	3.410856	0.0925
17	93	2	0.074230	0.545497	2.438973	1.077369	0.0925
149	76	3	0.149835	0.991542	6.293911	3.741891	0.0926
37	61	3	0.096917	0.574695	3.551582	2.478200	0.0926
108	76	4	0.066486	0.681446	8.874643	6.520876	0.0926
117	52	2	0.191996	0.959816	0.214059	5.811560	0.0926
40	54	3	0.109288	0.778913	9.021802	0.708567	0.0926
129	65	3	0.069800	0.851765	5.150564	0.671172	0.0926
126	50	3	0.104418	0.808189	9.780431	0.641345	0.0926

Figure 7. Autotuning Results for the Best 10 Models

13

Figure 8 plots the variable importance for the selected hyperparameter settings of the gradient boosting model. The two tree-based methods dominate.

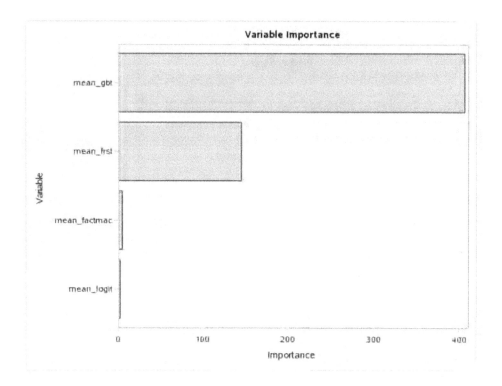

The following PROC GRADBOOST statements use the saved stacked ensemble model (cas.gbt_ensemble) to score the test set. The input data set (cas.test_mean_preds) includes Level-2 predictions for the test set.

```
proc gradboost data=cas.test_mean_preds inmodel=cas.gbt_ensemble;
    output out=cas.test_gbtscr copyvars=(id target);
run;
```

The following SAS code calculates the test ASE for the gradient boosting stacked ensemble model for the test data:

```
data cas.test_gbtscr;
    se=(p_target1-target)*(p_target1-target);
run;

proc cas;
    summary/ table={name='test_gbtscr', vars={'se'}};
run;
quit;
```

The **summary** action reports the ASE of the test data as 0.09298.

PROC GRADBOOST runs the **gbtreetrain** and **gbtreescore** CAS actions (in the Decision Tree action set) behind the scenes to train and score gradient boosting models. Appendix A provides a step-by-step CAS language (CASL) program that uses these actions to find the five-fold OOF predictions and cross validation ASE of the model for the hyperparameter values that are found here. Programming through CASL and CAS actions often requires more coding compared to using packaged machine learning procedures, which are essentially bundled functions of CAS actions. However, programming this way offers you more flexibility and control over the whole model building process. You can also call CAS actions through other languages such as Python and Lua.

HILL CLIMBING

The hill climbing technique (Caruana et al. 2004) is similar to forward stepwise selection. At each step of the selection, the model in the model library that maximizes the preferred performance metric joins the ensemble, and the ensemble is updated to be a simple weighted average of models. Hill climbing differs from regular stepwise selection in that rather than fitting a linear model at each step of the selection, it adds models to an ensemble by averaging predictions with the models already in the ensemble. As such, it is actually a form of nonnegative least squares, because the coefficients of each model are guaranteed to be nonnegative. Building an ensemble model this way can be very efficient computationally and has the significant advantage of being readily applicable to any performance metric of interest.

Caruana et al. (2004) use a hill climbing (single holdout validation) set at each step of the selection process to assess model performance. A separate validation set plays an important role in order to deal with overfitting, especially when you use the regular training predictions as input variables. However, instead of using a hill climbing validation set, this paper's analysis performs hill climbing on the library of OOF predictions. This approach deals with overfitting while maximally using the training data for the critical hill climbing step.

At each iteration of the hill climbing algorithm, every candidate model is evaluated to find the one that maximally improves the ensemble in a greedy fashion. Selection with replacement allows models to be added to the ensemble multiple times, permitting an already used model to be selected again rather than adding an unused model (which could possibly hurt the ensemble model's performance). Thus each model in the ensemble model can take different weights based on how many times it is selected.

For the Adult data, an ensemble model is built by using hill climbing for combining the four average Level-2 models. Figure 8 shows that the first model to enter the ensemble is the single best gradient boosted tree (gbt) model with a five-fold training cross validation ASE of 0.09235. Hill climbing keeps adding the same gradient boosting model until step 7. At step 7, the forest model joins the ensemble, which helps decrease both the training and testing errors nicely.

Obs	Step	Model	ASE_test	ASE_train		Obs	Step	Model	ASE_test	ASE_train
1	1	mean_gbt	0.092734	0.09235		10	10	mean_gbt	0.092678	0.09233
2	2	mean_gbt	0.092734	0.09235		11	11	mean_gbt	0.092679	0.09233
3	3	mean_gbt	0.092734	0.09235		12	12	mean_gbt	0.092680	0.09233
4	4	mean_gbt	0.092734	0.09235		13	13	mean_gbt	0.092682	0.09233
5	5	mean_gbt	0.092734	0.09235		14	14	mean_gbt	0.092684	0.09233
6	6	mean_gbt	0.092734	0.09235		15	15	mean_gbt	0.092685	0.09233
7	7	mean_frst	0.092684	0.09235		16	16	mean_gbt	0.092687	0.09233
8	8	mean_gbt	0.092679	0.09234		17	17	mean_gbt	0.092689	0.09233
9	9	mean_gbt	0.092678	0.09233		18	18	mean_gbt	0.092690	0.09233
10	10	mean_gbt	0.092678	0.09233		19	19	mean_gbt	0.092692	0.09233
						20	20	mean_gbt	0.092693	0.09233

Figure 8. First 20 Steps of Hill Climbing

Figure 9 shows graphically how the training and test errors change by the hill climbing steps. It shows that after step 9, the training error does not change much, but the test error increases slightly. The model at step 9 has a training ASE of 0.09268 and a testing ASE of 0.09233. If you choose this model at step9 as the final hill climbing model, the Level-2 average gradient boosting model takes a weight of 8, the Level-2 average forest model takes a weight of 1, and the other two models take 0 weights. In a typical hill climbing ensemble model, it is common to see powerful models being selected multiple times. In this case, the gbt model dominates but is complemented by a small contribution from forest model.

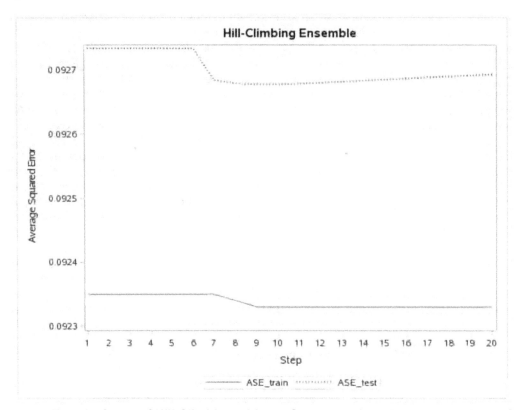

Figure 9. First 20 Steps of Hill Climbing with the Corresponding Training and Test ASEs

Because the hill climbing SAS program is lengthy, it is not provided here. See the GitHub repository for the full hill climbing program, which is written in the CAS language. The program is very flexible, and you can run it in the SAS Viya environment to build your own hill climbing ensemble model for your data.

When the same objective function is used, the nonnegative least squares approach is a generalization of hill climbing technique. For this example, Figure 10 shows that all three Level-3 linear modeling approaches (adaptive LASSO, nonnegative least squares, and hill climbing) produced very similar results and decreased the test ASE when compared to the single best model of Level-2 (shown in last row). On the other hand, the Level-3 stacked gradient boosting model did not provide a better model than the Level-2 average gradient boosting model.

Note that since the adaptive LASSO and the nonnegative least squares models weights are so close to each other, the training and test ASEs are almost the same when five decimal points are used. Note also that training ASEs are calculated when the Level-3 models are fit on the full training data.

Models	Training ASE	Test ASE
Level-3 adaptive LASSO	0.09269	0.09228
Level-3 nonnegative least squares	0.09269	0.09228
Level-3 gradient boosting	0.09130	0.09298
Level-3 hill climbing	0.09268	0.09233
Level-2 best model: average gradient boosting	**0.09236**	**0.09273**

Figure 10. Level-3 Stacked Models Training and Test ASEs Compared to the Single Best Level-2 Model

CONCLUSION

Stacked ensembling is an essential tool in any expert data scientist's toolbox. This paper shows how you can perform this valuable technique in the new SAS Viya framework by taking advantage of powerful underlying machine learning algorithms that are available through CAS procedures and actions.

REFERENCES

Breiman, L. 1995. "Stacked Regressions." *Machine Learning* 24:49–64.

Caruana, R., Niculescu-Mizil, A., Crew, G., and Ksikes, A. 2004. "Ensemble Selection from Libraries of Models." *Proceedings of the Twenty-First International Conference on Machine Learning.* New York: ACM.

Cawley, G. C., and Talbot, N. L. 2010. "On Over-fitting in Model Selection and Subsequent Selection Bias in Performance Evaluation." *Journal of Machine Learning Research* 11:2079–2107.

Dietterich, T. 2000. "Ensemble Methods in Machine Learning." *Lecture Notes in Computer Science* 1857:1–15.

Güneş, F. 2015. "Penalized Regression Methods for Linear Models in SAS/STAT." Cary, NC: SAS Institute Inc. Available at https://support.sas.com/rnd/app/stat/papers/2015/PenalizedRegression_LinearModels.pdf.

Hastie, T. J., Tibshirani, R. J., and Friedman, J. H. 2001. *The Elements of Statistical Learning: Data Mining, Inference, and Prediction.* New York: Springer-Verlag.

Koch, P., Wujek, B., Golovidov, O., and Gardner, S. 2017. "Automated Hyperparameter Tuning for Effective Machine Learning." In *Proceedings of the SAS Global Forum 2017 Conference.* Cary, NC: SAS Institute Inc. Available at http://support.sas.com/resources/papers/ proceedings17/SAS514-2017.pdf.

Lichman, M. 2013. UCI Machine Learning Repository. School of Information and Computer Sciences, University of California, Irvine. Available at http://archive.ics.uci.edu/ml.

Sill, J., Takacs, G., Mackey, L., and Lin, D. 2009. "Feature-Weighted Linear Stacking." CoRR abs/0911.0460.

Tibshirani, R. 1996. "Regression Shrinkage and Selection via the Lasso." *Journal of the Royal Statistical Society,* Series B 58:267–288.

Van der Laan, M. J., Polley, E. C., and Hubbard, A. E. 2007. "Super Learner." *U.C. Berkeley Division of Biostatistics Working Paper Series,* Working Paper 222.

Wexler, J., Haller, S., and Myneni, R. 2017. "An Overview of SAS Visual Data Mining and Machine Learning on SAS Viya." In *Proceedings of the SAS Global Forum 2017 Conference.* Cary, NC: SAS Institute Inc. Available at http://support.sas.com/resources/papers/ proceedings17/SAS1492-2017.pdf.

Wujek, B., Hall, P., and Güneş, F. 2016. "Best Practices in Machine Learning Applications." In *Proceedings of the SAS Global Forum 2016 Conference.* Cary, NC: SAS Institute Inc. Available at https://support.sas.com/resources/papers/proceedings16/SAS2360-2016.pdf.

Zou, H. 2006. "The Adaptive Lasso and Its Oracle Properties." *Journal of the American Statistical Association* 101:1418–1429.

ACKNOWLEDGMENTS

The authors are grateful to Wendy Czika and Padraic Neville of the Advanced Analytics Division of SAS for helpful comments and support. The authors also thank Anne Baxter for editorial assistance.

RECOMMENDED READING

A GitHub repository is available at https://github.com/sassoftware/sas-viya-machine-learning/stacking. The repository contains several different programs to help you reproduce results in this paper. The repository also contains supplemental material, including a detailed breakdown of some additional ensembling that is performed using Level-2 bootstrap samples.

Getting Started with SAS® Visual Data Mining and Machine Learning

SAS® Visual Data Mining and Machine Learning : Data Mining and Machine Learning Procedures

SAS® Visual Data Mining and Machine Learning : Statistical Procedures

SAS® Econometrics: Econometrical Procedures

SAS® Visual Data Mining and Machine Learning : Data Mining and Machine Learning Programming Guide

SAS® Cloud Analytic Services: CAS Procedure Programming Guide and Reference

CONTACT INFORMATION

Your comments and questions are valued and encouraged. Contact the authors:

Funda Güneş
SAS Institute Inc.
funda.gunes@sas.com

Russ Wolfinger
SAS Institute Inc.
Russ.Wolfinger@jmp.com

Pei-Yi Tan
SAS Institute Inc.
Pei-Yi.Tan@sas.com

APPENDIX A:

This appendix provides a step-by-step CAS language program that calculates and saves five-fold OOF predictions of the stacked ensemble model with the scalable gradient boosting algorithm for the set of hyperparameters that are shown in Figure 5. You can easily modify this program to obtain OOF predictions for your models that might use different machine learning training and scoring CAS actions.

```
/* Start a CAS session named mySession */
cas mySession;

/* Define a CAS engine libref for CAS in-memory data tables */
libname cas sasioca;

/* Create a SAS libref for the directory that has the data */
libname data "/folders/myfolders/";

/* Load OOF predictions into CAS using a DATA step */
data cas.train_oofs;
    set data.train_oofs;
    _fold_=int(ranuni(1)*5)+1;
run;

proc cas;
    /* Create an input variable list for modeling*/
    input_vars={{name='mean_gbt'},{name='mean_frst'},{name='mean_logit'},
                {name='mean_factmac'}};
    nFold=5;
```

```
    do i=1 to nFold;
        /* Generate no_fold_i and fold_i variables */
        no_fold_i = "_fold_ ne " || (String)i;
        fold_i    = "_fold_ eq " || (String)i;

        /* Generate a model name to store the ith trained model */
        mymodel = "gbt_" || (String)i;

        /* Generate a cas table name to store the scored data */
        scored_data = "gbtscore_" || (String)i;

        /* Train a gradient boosting model without fold i */
        decisiontree.gbtreetrain result=r1 /
            table={name='train_mean_oofs', where=no_fold_i}
            inputs=input_vars
            target="target"
            maxbranch=2
            maxlevel=5
            leafsize=60
            ntree=56
            m=3
            binorder=1
            nbins=100
            seed=1234
            subsamplerate=0.75938
            learningRate=0.10990
            lasso=3.25403
            ridge=3.64367
            casout={name=mymodel, replace=1};
            print r1;

        /* Score for the left out fold i */
        decisionTree.gbtreescore result = r2/
            table={name='train_mean_oofs', where=fold_i}
            model={name=mymodel}
            casout={name=scored_data, replace=TRUE }
            copyVars={"id", "target"}
            encodeName=true;
    end;
quit;

/* Put together OOF predictions */
data cas.gbt_stack_oofs (keep= id target p_target se);
    set cas.gbtscore_1-cas.gbtscore_5;
    se=(p_target-target)*(p_target-target);
    run;
run;

/* The mean value for variable se is the 5-fold cross validation error */
proc cas;
    summary / table={name='gbt_stack_oofs', vars={'se'}};
run;
/* Quit PROC CAS */
quit;
```

Paper SAS118-2017

DATA Step in SAS® Viya™: Essential New Features

Jason Secosky, SAS Institute Inc., Cary, NC

ABSTRACT

The DATA step is the familiar and powerful data processing language in SAS® and now SAS Viya™. The DATA step's simple syntax provides row-at-a-time operations to edit, restructure, and combine data. New to the DATA step in SAS Viya are a varying-length character data type and parallel execution. Varying-length character data enables intuitive string operations that go beyond the 32KB limit of current DATA step operations. Parallel execution speeds the processing of big data by starting the DATA step on multiple machines and dividing data processing among threads on these machines. To avoid multi-threaded programming errors, the run-time environment for the DATA step is presented along with potential programming pitfalls. Come see how the DATA step in SAS Viya makes your data processing simpler and faster.

INTRODUCTION

The DATA step is a programming language to prepare tables for analysis. It excels at modifying existing values and computing new values in a row, as well as combining tables. In SAS, a DATA step runs in a single thread or core on your system.

This is where our problem lies. With big data, running in a single thread is slow. Some DATA steps can take hours to complete. With SAS Cloud Analytics Services (CAS) in SAS Viya, we have an environment where tens or hundreds of threads are available, across several machines. When you program your DATA steps to run in CAS, all of those threads become available for you to use to improve the performance with massive parallel processing.

For detailed information about CAS, please refer to *SAS® Cloud Analytic Services 3.1: Fundamentals*. A link to this document is in the Resources section of this paper.

RUNNING A DATA STEP IN PARALLEL IN CAS

How do you program your DATA steps to run in CAS? In many ways, you program just like you would in SAS, taking advantage of your experience as a SAS programmer. Where DATA steps run is driven by where your tables are stored. If your tables are stored in SAS, the DATA step runs in SAS. If your tables are stored in CAS, the DATA step runs in CAS. If the tables are in a mix of locations, then the DATA step runs in SAS. Running "in SAS" means the DATA step runs on the SAS client, not in CAS.

In this paper, we inspect several DATA steps, learn where they run (in SAS or in CAS), and understand how running in a single thread in SAS is different from running in many threads in CAS.

Below is a figure of what it looks like to run DATA steps in CAS. In this diagram, a table is stored in CAS and several threads of a DATA step operate on the table. The same DATA step program runs in each thread.

How does running the same program in each thread improve performance? CAS splits up the table so that each thread independently works on part of the table. Splitting the table among threads is where our parallelism and speedup come from. Instead of having one thread work on the entire table, you have many threads, each working on part of the table.

1

Running the DATA Step in SAS Cloud Analytic Services (CAS)

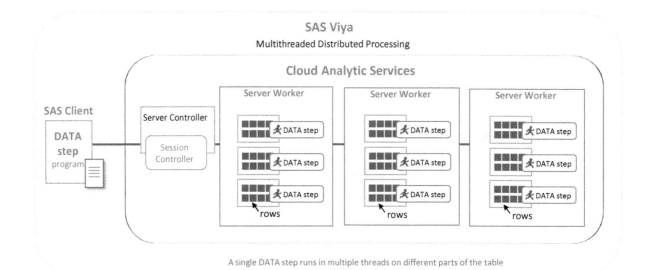

A single DATA step runs in multiple threads on different parts of the table

Figure 1. DATA Step Running in SAS Cloud Analytic Services (CAS)

In the next sections, we look at common DATA steps for preparing data sets for analytics. For most of these examples, we run a DATA step in SAS then modify the DATA step to run in CAS. The DATA steps we run perform these actions:

- Print "hello world" from each thread

- Load a table from SAS into CAS

- Compute a new variable value for each row

- Sum a value across an entire table

- Sum a value for BY groups within the data

- Operate on varying-length character data

PRINT "HELLO WORLD" FROM EACH THREAD

In this example, we run a program that prints a "hello" message from SAS and then CAS.

```
/* "Hello World" in SAS */
data _null_;
   put 'Hello world from ' _threadid_=;
run;

/* Create a CAS session to run DATA step in */
cas casauto;

/* "Hello World" in CAS */
data _null_ / sessref=casauto;
   put 'Hello world from ' _threadid_=;
run;
```

```
61        /* "Hello World" in SAS */
62        data _null_;
63           put 'Hello world from ' _threadid_=;
64        run;
```

```
Hello world from _THREADID_=1

65
66          /* Create a CAS session to run DATA step in */
67          cas casauto;
68
69          /* "Hello World" in CAS */
70          data _null_ / sessref=casauto;
71              put 'Hello world from ' _threadid_=;
72          run;
NOTE: Running DATA step in Cloud Analytic Services.
Hello world from _THREADID_=9
Hello world from _THREADID_=2
Hello world from _THREADID_=4
Hello world from _THREADID_=5
Hello world from _THREADID_=8
Hello world from _THREADID_=6
Hello world from _THREADID_=3
Hello world from _THREADID_=10
Hello world from _THREADID_=1
Hello world from _THREADID_=11
Hello world from _THREADID_=15
Hello world from _THREADID_=12
Hello world from _THREADID_=14
Hello world from _THREADID_=16
Hello world from _THREADID_=7
Hello world from _THREADID_=13
```

Output 1. "Hello World" Running in Several Threads

Notice the new automatic variable, _THREADID_, in the DATA step in SAS Viya. This variable is filled with the thread number of the thread running the DATA step. Thread numbers start at 1 and go up to N, where N is the maximum number of threads available.

In the program that runs in SAS, there is one-line output because only one thread is used.

In the program that runs in CAS, the note indicates the program ran in CAS. The next set of lines shows the program running in all available threads. There are 16 threads available, each runs the same program, so each outputs a line to the log. If you run the CAS program multiple times, you will see the output is in a different order. Why would the output be in a different order?

All of the threads operate independently. This means log messages are generated by each thread at slightly different times, resulting in slightly different ordering for each run. If the DATA step were to somehow synchronize the output of log messages, we would lose the performance gain that threads give.

Remember we said the DATA step runs in CAS if the tables that it operates on are stored in CAS? This program does not operate on any tables, so we have to use the SESSREF= option in the DATA statement to force the DATA step to run in CAS. Without the SESSREF= option, the DATA step runs in SAS.

In this first example, we have seen a DATA step running in SAS in a single thread and the same DATA step running in CAS in multiple threads. Each thread operates independently, so there is no ordering of the thread output.

LOAD A TABLE FROM SAS INTO CAS

In this example, we load a SAS data set into a CAS table using two methods. The first is a DATA step using the CAS engine. The second uses the LOAD statement of the CASUTIL Procedure.

```
/* Setup libraries we are going to use */
```

```
/* One for SAS data, one for CAS data */
libname sas '<path-to-data-sets>';
libname cas cas;

/* Load table into CAS with DATA step and the CAS engine */
data cas.purchase;
   set sas.purchase;
run;

/* Load table into CAS with PROC CASUTIL */
proc casutil;
  load data=sas.purchase casout="purchase" replace;
quit;
```

```
62            /* Load table into CAS with DATA step and the CAS engine */
63            data cas.purchase;
64               set sas.purchase;
65            run;

NOTE: There were 192735 observations read from the data set SAS.PURCHASE.
NOTE: The data set CAS.PURCHASE has 192735 observations and 19 variables.
NOTE: DATA statement used (Total process time):
      real time              0.17 seconds
      cpu time               0.08 seconds

66
67            /* Load table into CAS with PROC CASUTIL */
68            proc casutil;
NOTE: The UUID '369001c7-acce-4644-bee7-bd24cfd743a1' is connected
      using session CASAUTO.
69               load data=sas.purchase casout="purchase" replace;
NOTE: SAS.PURCHASE was successfully added to the "CASUSER(<userid>)"
      caslib as "purchase".
70            quit;

NOTE: PROCEDURE CASUTIL used (Total process time):
      real time              0.21 seconds
      cpu time               0.09 seconds
```

Output 2. Two Ways to Load Data into CAS

In this example, the DATA step and PROC CASUTIL perform the same operation. When would you select one over the other? Both DATA step and PROC CASUTIL support selecting rows and columns to add to the new table. If more data processing needs to occur while loading, the DATA step can be used to load and transform with one step. If additional processing is not necessary, the intent of loading data is clearer when using the LOAD statement with PROC CASUTIL.

Also notice when the DATA step completes, there is no message about running the DATA step in CAS. Because the input table is stored in a SAS library and not in CAS, the DATA step runs in SAS.

COMPUTING A NEW VARIABLE

With a table loaded into CAS, we can perform some operations on it. In this example, we create a new variable, CUST_ACTIVITY, whose values are *High*, *Medium*, *Low*, or *Unknown*, based on one of the categorical variables, CAT_INPUT1. The program first runs in SAS, then we change the DATA step to run in CAS by changing the librefs to indicate the data are stored in CAS.

The program also writes to the log the number of rows each thread operates on. This diagnostic message helps us to understand how each thread operates on the part of data assigned to it.

```
/* Use DATA step to transform a value in a row */
/* Run in both SAS and CAS to see how many rows each thread processes */

/* SAS */
data sas.purchase_activity;
   length cust_activity $ 8;

   set sas.purchase end=done;

 /* Transform value */
   select (cat_input1);
   when ('X') cust_activity = 'High';
   when ('Y') cust_activity = 'Medium';
   when ('Z') cust_activity = 'Low';
   otherwise  cust_activity = 'Unknown';
   end;

 /* Output number rows this thread processed */
   if done then
      put _threadid_=z2. _N_=;
run;

/* CAS */
/* To run in CAS, SAS librefs changed to CAS librefs. */
data cas.purchase_activity;
   length cust_activity $ 8;

   set cas.purchase end=done;

 /* Transform value */
   select (cat_input1);
   when ('X') cust_activity = 'High';
   when ('Y') cust_activity = 'Medium';
   when ('Z') cust_activity = 'Low';
   otherwise  cust_activity = 'Unknown';
   end;

 /* Output number rows this thread processed */
   if done then
      put _threadid_=z2. _N_=;
run;
```

```
60          /* SAS */
61          data sas.purchase_activity;
62             length cust_activity $ 8;
63
64             set sas.purchase end=done;
65
66           /* Transform value */
67             select (cat_input1);
68             when ('X') cust_activity = 'High';
69             when ('Y') cust_activity = 'Medium';
70             when ('Z') cust_activity = 'Low';
71             otherwise  cust_activity = 'Unknown';
```

```
72                   end;
73
74             /* Output number rows this thread processed */
75               if done then
76                  put _threadid_=z2. _N_=;
77           run;

_THREADID_=01 _N_=192735
NOTE: There were 192735 observations read from the data set SAS.PURCHASE.
NOTE: The data set SAS.PURCHASE_ACTIVITY has 192735 observations
      and 20 variables.
NOTE: DATA statement used (Total process time):
      real time           0.25 seconds
      cpu time            0.10 seconds


78
79           /* CAS */
80           /* To run in CAS, SAS librefs changed to CAS librefs. */
81           data cas.purchase_activity;
82              length cust_activity $ 8;
83
84              set cas.purchase end=done;
85
86            /* Transform value */
87              select (cat_input1);
88              when ('X') cust_activity = 'High';
89              when ('Y') cust_activity = 'Medium';
90              when ('Z') cust_activity = 'Low';
91              otherwise  cust_activity = 'Unknown';
92              end;
93
94            /* Output number rows this thread processed */
95              if done then
96                 put _threadid_=z2. _N_=;
97           run;

NOTE: Running DATA step in Cloud Analytic Services.
NOTE: The DATA step will run in multiple threads.
_THREADID_=07 _N_=12000
_THREADID_=11 _N_=12000
_THREADID_=09 _N_=12000
_THREADID_=08 _N_=12000
_THREADID_=12 _N_=12000
_THREADID_=03 _N_=12000
_THREADID_=16 _N_=11735
_THREADID_=04 _N_=12000
_THREADID_=05 _N_=12000
_THREADID_=02 _N_=12000
_THREADID_=13 _N_=12000
_THREADID_=01 _N_=13000
_THREADID_=14 _N_=12000
_THREADID_=15 _N_=12000
_THREADID_=06 _N_=12000
_THREADID_=10 _N_=12000
NOTE: There were 192735 observations read from the table PURCHASE
```

```
             in caslib CASUSER(<userid>).
  NOTE: The table purchase_activity in caslib CASUSER(<userid>) has
        192735 observations and 20 variables.
  NOTE: DATA statement used (Total process time):
        real time              0.08 seconds
        cpu time               0.02 seconds
```

Output 3. Adding a New Variable

To run the DATA step in CAS, the data was loaded into CAS and the only modification made to the DATA step is to change the librefs used to CAS librefs. Because the bulk of the program remains intact, you can reuse your SAS programming experience to write DATA steps that run in parallel in CAS.

When the DATA step runs in CAS, notice how some threads are assigned a few more rows to operate on and some threads a few less. Although CAS does a good job trying to evenly distribute the input rows among threads, some threads might get a few more and some might get a few less than others. With small data, some threads might process no rows at all.

Also, notice how even this small data program sees an improvement in performance because the work was split up among several threads.

In these examples, we see by changing the librefs used in the program to be CAS librefs, the program runs in multiple threads in CAS. Otherwise, the program runs in SAS. We also see how the PUT statement can be used to give debugging feedback on where the program runs and the number of rows a thread processes.

TWO-STEP OPERATIONS

So far, transforming a single-threaded DATA step to run in multiple threads has been a simple transformation. Unfortunately, you cannot take any DATA step, change the librefs used, and have it run correctly in parallel. You still have to know what your program is doing to make sure you know what it does when it runs in parallel.

In this example, we sum a variable across all the rows of a table. The RETAIN statement tells the DATA step to hold a value from one row to the next without resetting it to missing. When running a DATA step in CAS, our first attempt is to only change the librefs to CAS librefs and we discover that while this gets us close to a solution, it isn't a complete solution. We have to be careful with retained variables because each thread retains the values that it sees. When you use a retained variable to hold a sum, the variable will contain the sum of the values that that thread sees.

```
/* Sum a variable across an entire table */

/* SAS */
/* Retain a variable to sum the number of homeowners over all rows */
data sas.sums;
   retain homeowners_sum;
   keep homeowners_sum;

   set sas.purchase end=done;

   if demog_ho = 1 then
      homeowners_sum + 1;

   if done then
      output;
run;

title 'DATA Step in SAS';
proc print data=sas.sums; run;
```

```
/* CAS */
/* Partial sums computed by threads */
data cas.sums;
    retain homeowners_sum;
    keep homeowners_sum;

    set cas.purchase end=done;

    if demog_ho = 1 then
        homeowners_sum + 1;

    if done then
        output;
run;

title 'DATA Step in CAS';
proc print data=cas.sums; run;
```

DATA Step in SAS

Obs	homeowners_sum
1	106054

DATA Step in CAS

Obs	homeowners_sum
1	7500
2	6563
3	7238
4	7391
5	6966
6	7278
7	7125
8	6822
9	6709
10	7276
11	6760
12	6262
13	4774
14	6787
15	5999
16	4604

Output 4. Multiple Threads Output Multiple Rows in CAS

When the DATA step runs in CAS, we see 16 rows of output instead of 1 as we do in SAS. This happens because each thread sums the values that it reads and generates the partial sum that it computed. In this case, 16 threads read data, so we see 16 rows of output. In some sense, this is what we want, to keep all the threads busy computing the sum of the rows they are assigned. To get one final sum, we need something new.

What we need is a way to gather all the partial sum rows and bring them to a single thread. This single thread can sum the partial sums to give a final sum. To do this, a new option is used in the DATA statement, SINGLE=.

When SINGLE=YES is specified, the DATA step runs in a single thread instead of all available threads. When SINGLE=NO is specified, the DATA step runs in all available threads. The default if SINGLE= is not specified is SINGLE=NO, which causes the DATA step runs in all available threads. Here is the program using SINGLE=YES to produce a final sum.

```
/* Use the SINGLE=YES option to run DATA step in a single thread */
data cas.sums_all / single=yes;
   retain homeowners_sum_all;
   keep homeowners_sum_all;

   set cas.sums end=done;

   homeowners_sum_all + homeowners_sum;

   if done then
      output;
run;

title 'Final Sum';
proc print data=cas.sums_all; run;
```

Final Sum

Obs	homeowners_sum_all
1	106054

Output 5. Using SINGLE=YES to Run DATA Step in One Thread

Using SINGLE=YES is convenient when needing a short serial section in a multi-threaded program. If a DATA step with SINGLE=YES processes large tables, not only does the program run slowly by operating in a single thread, the machine executing the single thread can run out of disk or memory resources. Use SINGLE=YES with caution.

While this program uses RETAIN to hold a value from row to row, there are additional features in the DATA step that create dependencies between rows. These are the LAG and DIF functions and temporary arrays. If your program uses these, then a two-step solution might be needed.

This example highlights that each thread has its own variables and computes based on the values that it reads. Because there is no sharing between the threads, we had to break the single DATA step that ran in SAS into two DATA steps that run in CAS. One DATA step runs in parallel on the big data and one runs in a single thread on smaller data. This solution speeds processing by running as much as possible in multiple threads.

BY-GROUP PROCESSING

So far, we have seen row-at-a-time processing: one row in, modify some variables, and one row out. Another useful form of programming is BY-group processing, where rows with the same BY value are grouped together and processed by a single thread.

To process BY groups in a DATA step, you use the SORT procedure to group rows by the BY variables. After the rows are grouped, the BY statement in the DATA step creates special FIRST. and LAST. variables to detect the start and end of each BY group. The BY statement also allows rows to be interleaved or combined with the SET or MERGE statement.

When running a DATA step in CAS, everything is the same, except you do not sort the data before running the DATA step. When using a BY statement in a DATA step in CAS, CAS groups and orders the

9

data on the fly, and complete BY groups are given to a thread for processing. With multiple threads, multiple BY groups are processed at the same time.

In this example, we sum a variable for a BY group. The result is one sum per BY group. This example is not as complex as summing across an entire table because one thread processes an entire BY group. Therefore, one thread can do the summing within a BY group. There is no need for two DATA steps.

```
/* Sum a variable for each BY group */

/* SAS */
/* Sort table and then we can use BY statement in DATA step */
proc sort data=sas.purchase;
   by cat_input2;
run;

data sas.sum_by_group;
   keep cat_input2 purch_sum;

   set sas.purchase;
   by cat_input2;

   if first.cat_input2 then
      purch_sum = 0;

  /* Sum purchase average for each profitability category */
  purch_sum + purchavgall;

   if last.cat_input2 then
      output;
run;

title 'DATA Step in SAS';
proc print data=sas.sum_by_group; run;

/* CAS */
data cas.sum_by_group;
   keep cat_input2 purch_sum;

   set cas.purchase;
   by cat_input2;

   if first.cat_input2 then
      purch_sum = 0;

   /* Sum purchase average for each profitability category */
   purch_sum + purchavgall;

   if last.cat_input2 then
      output;
run;

title 'DATA Step in CAS';
proc print data=cas.sum_by_group; run;
```

DATA Step in SAS

Obs	cat_input2	purch_sum
1	A	500058.68

Obs	cat_input2	purch_sum
2	B	433806.88
3	C	384411.25
4	D	382550.10
5	E	872475.33

DATA Step in CAS

Obs	cat_input2	purch_sum
1	A	500058.68
2	C	384411.25
3	B	433806.88
4	E	872475.33
5	D	382550.10

Output 6. BY-Group Processing in DATA Step

When the DATA step runs in SAS, one thread performs the BY-group sum, and rows are in the order in which the single thread encounters them in the input.

When the DATA step runs in CAS, the BY statement tells the DATA step to request that the data are grouped on the first BY variable from CAS. CAS groups the data and entire groups are given to a thread. With multiple threads DATA step processes multiple BY groups at the same time.

Performance is affected by the cardinality of the first BY variable. Too few BY values and threads sit idle. Too many BY values and the overhead of grouping becomes a factor.

Grouping rows in CAS does take time. If you are expecting to do a lot of BY processing on a table, you can use the CAS procedure to invoke the Partition action to pre-partition a table before using it. The LOAD statement in the CASUTIL procedure also has options to partition a table when loading the data.

Another popular use of the DATA step is to merge two or more tables with a MERGE statement. Merging BY groups also occurs in parallel. I encourage you to try it when you have access to SAS Viya.

We have seen BY-group processing in a DATA step in CAS. There is no need to sort the data before using a BY statement and multiple BY groups are operated on in parallel by different threads.

VARYING-LENGTH CHARACTER VARIABLES

Character variables in SAS are fixed width. This means if a variable is declared to have a length of 1024, 1024 bytes of memory are used and 1024 bytes of disk space per row are used. If the value does not use all 1024 bytes, the value is blank-padded.

Operations on fixed-width variables can be fast because you are guaranteed to always have a certain number of bytes available. Unfortunately, they can use more space than is needed and are not intuitive to program with for some programmers.

To save memory and have more intuitive string operations, we have added a varying-length character type, or varchar for short, to both SAS and CAS.

Varchar variables are given a maximum width, and space is allocated as needed up to the maximum. Shorter values take less space than longer values and values are not blank padded. Also, the length of a varchar value can go beyond the current 32KB limit for character variables in SAS. In a DATA step, varchar values can be up to 2GB in size.

This might seem like a win-win-win combination. Unfortunately, to manage varying-length values, more instructions are needed when operating with varchar variables. The hope is that additional time is made up by reduced I/O time and memory use.

In this set of examples, we see how varchar variables are more intuitive to work with than character variables. We see how string concatenation is simpler without blank padding. Then, we see how character variables are measured in units of bytes, whereas varchar variables are measured in units of characters. Using units of characters is more intuitive with non-English characters or symbols that take multiple bytes.

```
/* Use varying-length character variables (varchar) in a DATA step */
/* More intuitive operations -- no longer need to remove trailing blanks */
/* Before varchar, had to trim trailing blanks to get needed result */

data _null_;
    length first last $ 32 fullname_notrim fullname $ 64;

    first = "Jane";
    last = "Jones";
    fullname_notrim = first || ' ' || last;
    fullname = trim(first) || ' ' || last;

    put fullname_notrim=;
    put fullname=;
run;

/* No trailing blanks with varchar, more intuitive operations */
data _null_;
    length first last fullname varchar(*);

    first = "Jane";
    last = "Jones";
    fullname = first || ' ' || last;

    put fullname=;
run;

/* Find length of a string */
/* Character values are measured in units of bytes */
/* Varchar are measured in units of characters */
data _null_;
    length c $ 64;
    length vc varchar(*);

    c  = "谢谢为使用SAS!";

    vc = "谢谢为使用SAS!";

    c_len = length(c);
    vc_len = length(vc);

    put c_len= vc_len=;
run;
```

```
61          data _null_;
62              length first last $ 32 fullname_notrim fullname $ 64;
63
64              first = "Jane";
65              last = "Jones";
66              fullname_notrim = first || ' ' || last;
67              fullname = trim(first) || ' ' || last;
```

```
68
69              put fullname_notrim=;
70              put fullname=;
71          run;

fullname_notrim=Jane                              Jones
fullname=Jane Jones
NOTE: DATA statement used (Total process time):
      real time          0.00 seconds
      cpu time           0.01 seconds


72
73          /* No trailing blanks with varchar, more intuitive operations */
74          data _null_;
75              length first last fullname varchar(*);
76
77              first = "Jane";
78              last = "Jones";
79              fullname = first || ' ' || last;
80
81              put fullname=;
82          run;

fullname=Jane Jones
NOTE: DATA statement used (Total process time):
      real time          0.00 seconds
      cpu time           0.01 seconds


83
84          /* Find length of a string */
85          /* Character values are measured in units of bytes */
86          /* Varchar are measured in units of characters */
87          data _null_;
88              length c $ 64;
89              length vc varchar(*);
90
91              c  = "谢谢为使用SAS!";

92              vc = "谢谢为使用SAS!";

93
94              c_len = length(c);
95              vc_len = length(vc);
96
97              put c_len= vc_len=;
98          run;

c_len=19 vc_len=9
NOTE: DATA statement used (Total process time):
      real time          0.00 seconds
      cpu time           0.01 seconds
```

Output 7. Varchar Use in DATA Step

In the first program, the blank padding of fixed-width character values is not so intuitive. To remove the blank padding, we have to use the TRIM function or call one of the CAT functions to perform the concatenation.

In the second program, varchar variables are used. There is no blank padding, and the concatenation operator produces the value we might expect without having to use additional functions.

In the third program, five Chinese characters are used. Each Chinese character uses three bytes. Although the character variable holds four Chinese characters and five Latin characters, the LENGTH function reports 19 bytes are used. When using a varchar variable to hold the same value, the LENGTH function reports nine characters are used, even though the value uses 19 bytes.

Other functions, like the SUBSTR and INDEX functions, also use numbers in units of characters instead of bytes when passed varchar variables. Using a unit of characters is more intuitive when processing multiple types of languages.

CONCLUSION

We have explored running the DATA step in CAS. Understanding when the DATA step runs in SAS and when it runs in CAS is important in knowing how the DATA step operates. While changing SAS librefs to CAS librefs can get many programs to run faster in multiple threads in CAS, other programs require more thought and might need to be broken into two steps instead of one. In exchange for this effort, running DATA step in multiple threads can greatly reduce the time to process large tables.

ACKNOWLEDGMENTS

Developing software is a team effort. I would like to thank those involved in the development, testing, documentation, and support of DATA step in CAS: David Bultman, Melissa Corn, Hua Rui Dong, Jerry Pendergrass, Denise Poll, Mike Jones, Lisa Davenport, Jane Eslinger, Kevin Russell, Al Kulik, Rick Langston, Kanthi Yedavalli, Joe Slater, Robert Ray, Mark Gass, and Oliver Schabenberger. Thanks to David Bultman, Lisa Davenport, Jane Eslinger, Kevin Russell, and Julia Schelly for reviewing this paper.

RESOURCES

- SAS Institute Inc. 2017. *SAS® Cloud Analytic Services 3.1: Fundamentals.* Available at http://go.documentation.sas.com/?docsetId=casfun&docsetVersion=3.1&docsetTarget=titlepage.htm.

- SAS Institute Inc. 2017. *SAS® Visual Data Mining and Machine Learning 8.1, Accessing and Manipulating Data, Data Step Programming.* Available at http://go.documentation.sas.com/?cdcId=vdmmlcdc&cdcVersion=8.1&docsetId=casdataam&docsetTarget=p0qlpqt6uhyqhen17qyj6mc9shtp.htm.

- *Accelerating SAS DATA Step Performance with SAS Viya.* Available at http://support.sas.com/training/tutorial/viya/viyavsp01.html.

CONTACT INFORMATION

Your comments and questions are valued and encouraged. Contact the author:

Jason Secosky
100 SAS Campus Drive
Cary, NC 27513
SAS Institute Inc.
Jason.Secosky@sas.com
http://www.sas.com

SAS 758-2017

An Introduction to SAS® Visual Analytics 8.1

Jeff Diamond, SAS Institute Inc.

ABSTRACT

The first release of SAS® Visual Analytics version 8.1 on SAS® Viya™ has something exciting for everyone. The latest version is a clean, modern HTML5 interface. SAS® Visual Analytics Designer, SAS® Visual Analytics Explorer, and SAS® Visual Statistics are merged into a single web application. Whether you are designing reports, exploring data or running interactive, predictive models, it is all integrated into one seamless experience. The application delivers on the same basic promise: get pertinent answers from any-size data. This paper will walk you through key features that you have come count on from auto charting to display rules and more. It will acclimate you to the new interface and highlight a few exciting new features like web content and donut pie charts. Finally, this paper will touch upon the ability to promote your existing reports to the new environment.

INTRODUCTION

This paper will serve as an introduction to SAS® Visual Analytics 8.1 (VA). It is the tenth release of the software and the first release on SAS® Viya™. The interface has been completely rewritten in HTML5. It is a clean, modern interface we hope you will enjoy. In addition, we took this opportunity to merge SAS® Visual Analytics Designer and SAS® Visual Analytics Explorer into a single application. The add-on SAS® Visual Statistics is also fully integrated into this new web application. There is more. SAS® Visual Data Mining and Machine Learning is also available as a fully integrated add-on. SAS Visual Analytics gives you a one stop shop for all your interactive data exploration, modeling, and reporting.

SAS® Visual Analytics

Get pertinent answers from any-size data. Smart data exploration makes it clear. Interactive reporting makes it collaborative. Self-service analytics makes it usable by anyone. And scalability and governance make it the perfect fit.

SAS® Viya™

From the world leader in analytics comes a modern, open platform that conquers analytics challenges – from experimental to mission-critical. SAS Viya is a single, cloud-ready environment that serves everyone – from data scientists to business analysts, application developers to executives – with the reliable, scalable, secure analytics management and governance essential for agile IT.

CLEAN, MODERN INTERFACE

The application has been completely rewritten in HTML5. The visual design is very different; however, the user interface builds upon elements that are familiar to current users of SAS Visual Analytics. It is worth taking a tour.

Current users of SAS Visual Analytics will immediately recognize the three pane design. The left pane (3) contains Data, Objects and an Outline view that is new for 8.1. Your report (4) is in the center. The right pane contains Options, Roles, Actions, Rules, Filters, and Ranks (5).

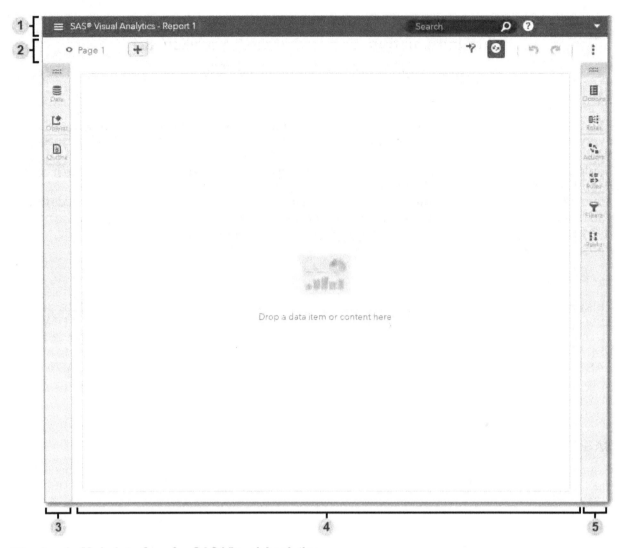

Display 1. Main Interface for SAS Visual Analytics

There are a few twists to the core three pane design. The left and right panes can be pinned or unpinned. An unpinned pane will automatically open when selected and disappear when an operation is complete. A pinned pane can be collapsed and expanded, but will remain expanded while in use. Either pane may be pinned or unpinned. By default, the left pane is unpinned and the right pane is pinned. Adventurous users can also tear off the panes or place them adjacent to one another. In today's world screen sizes vary greatly and these panes will adapt to meet your needs.

Your report takes center stage and the application's interface is designed to be as unobtrusive as possible; there when you need it and in the background when you do not.

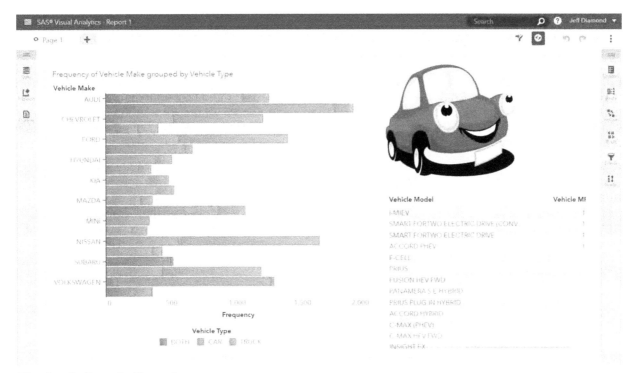

Display 2. Sample Report

Anyone who uses SAS Visual Analytics for 5 minutes will want to add objects and data to a report. To add objects to a report you open the objects pane on the left. SAS Visual Analytics offers a few dozen different types of objects. Click on the object you would like to add and drag it onto the canvas. There will be a blue box or line that indicates where the object will be added.

Display 3. Drop Zone for Report Object

If you did not choose data when prompted by the Welcome Dialog, then you will need to first select a data source. To do this you can open the Data pane.

Once you have added your data table you will want add data to your report. This can work in two ways. If you wish for SAS Visual Analytics to automatically choose the best chart for your data, then you can select one or more data items of interest and drag them to the report. At first your report canvas will be empty and the first object will be added. SAS Visual Analytics will choose the best chart, but if you prefer a different choice it's easy to change.

If you want to add more data, you will need to think about whether to add the data to an object that's already in the report or whether to create a new object. If you want to add the data item to an object already in the report then drag it to the center of the object. When you see a big blue box let go to add the data item. Alternatively, if you prefer to add a new object based on the data item then drag it to the left, right, top, or bottom of the object. You will see a blue line indicating where the new object will be added.

Display 4. Add Data to Report Object

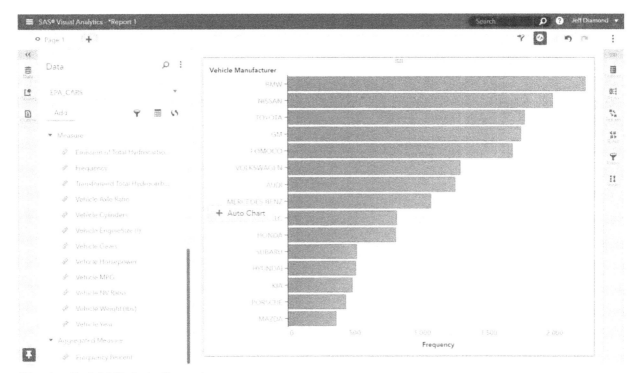

Display 5. Add Data to Report

There are many tasks you can initiate from the data pane: add or manage data sources, hierarchies, calculated items, custom categories, parameters, global filters and more. This paper will not cover these tasks in detail. You may also view or modify attributes of each data item.

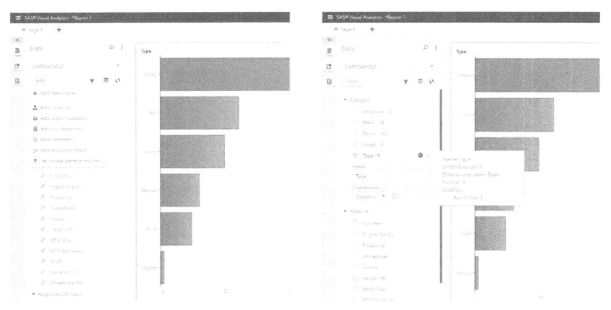

Display 6. Data Pane

The objects pane contains a robust set of choices ranging from essential data visualization objects to objects tailored for reporting and modeling. You may find that some of the objects near the bottom appear gray. The application is called SAS Visual Analytics, but in order to offer you a seamless, interactive experience the application encompasses objects that are part of the SAS Visual Analytics bundle as well as the SAS Visual Statistics and SAS Visual Data Mining and Machine Learning bundles. Please contact your account executive if these objects are of interest to you.

The outline pane is new in 8.1. It acts like a table of contents for your report and provides an overview of the pages and objects within the report. You can also rename or move object and pages from within this pane.

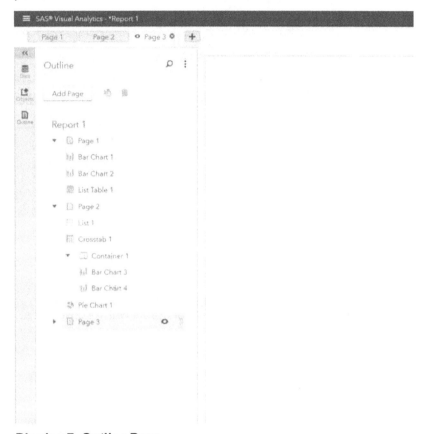

Display 7. Outline Pane

The right pane contains various elements that apply to the selected object. These will be familiar to you if you are a current SAS Visual Analytics user. However, a few of the names have changed. There is a wealth of product capabilities within each these panes, but this paper will not cover them in detail. Each type of object has an associated set of options that can be set. In SAS Visual Analytics 8.1 the "properties" and "styles" have been organized together in the Options pane. The Roles pane allows fine-grained control of how the data is assigned to the objects. This pane also supports drag and drop from the Data pane or between roles within pane. The Actions pane used to be referred to as Interactions, but it retains the same purpose. It was renamed to avoid confusion with statistical interactions. You can define page and report links from this pane. You can also add filter and linked selection actions between objects. Display rules, or more simply Rules, allows you to visually format an object based upon the value of a particular category or measure. Finally, the Filter and Rank panes allow robust control of the data query that's associated with the selected object.

One final note about the objects. Every object also contains a toolbar which allows you to perform many other actions such as export data, add a title, change the type of the object, and many more.

Display 8. Object Toolbar

Now that you are oriented to the left, middle, and right side of the application there is only one part that remains, the top.

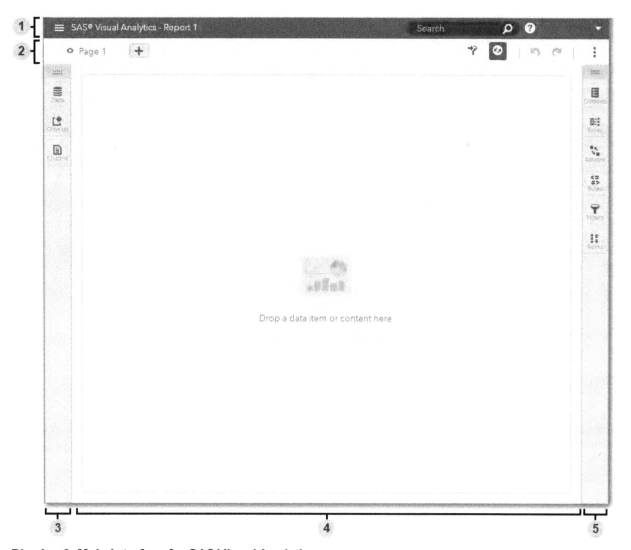

Display 9. Main Interface for SAS Visual Analytics

The banner (1), a blue bar across the top, is common across SAS web applications. The side menu is invoked from the "hamburger" (three horizontal white bars) in the top left. It will allow you to easily navigate to other SAS applications you have access to use. There is a terrific Help Center available on the banner as well.

Just below the banner is a toolbar where there are a number of application tasks to get familiar with (2). You can add, reorder, rename and delete pages in your report.

The report and page prompt bars can be quickly expanded or collapsed via the ⇗ on this toolbar. These prompt bars are an efficient way to filter all the objects in a page or report.

There is also a 🌐 to temporarily disable queries. This can be useful if you have several compute intensive settings to perform. This is more common when modeling your data.

You will not miss the ↩ and ↪. To the right of these buttons there are a number of options in the overflow menu including Save.

MERGING OF APPLICATIONS

Whatever your task SAS Visual Analytics aims to make it feel natural. You can move seamlessly between data exploration, reporting, and modeling.

SAS Visual Analytics lets you work the way you want to work. When you load SAS Visual Analytics you will see the Welcome Dialog which Invites you to choose data, open an existing report, or start with a blank report that does not contain data. You can make any of these options the default and opt to skip this step in the future. The purpose is to allow you to choose how you work. Some users want to get straight to the data while other users may build out the layout and visuals in their report before assigning data.

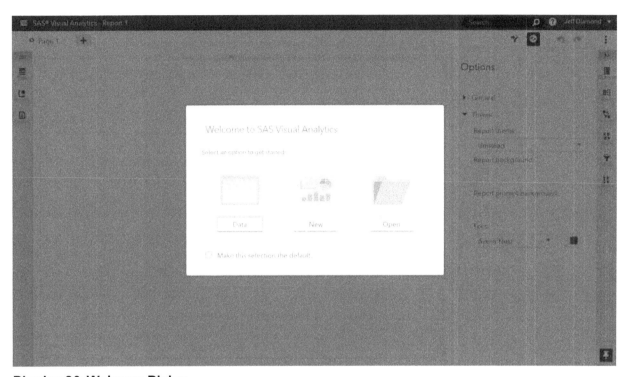

Display 20. Welcome Dialog

In SAS Visual Analytics all objects work seamlessly alongside one another. Previously, objects like a histogram or box plot were available only within SAS Visual Analytics Explorer (Explorer). These objects can be added directly into your report and will participate as targets of filter actions. The limitations that were present when exporting objects from the Explorer to SAS Visual Analytics Designer (Designer) are no longer present.

The benefits go in both directions. Operations found only in the Explorer can now be applied to objects that were found only in the Designer. For example, the ability to change the type of an object extends to traditional reporting objects like a pie chart. The auto charting logic found in the Explorer is also present in SAS Visual Analytics and is expanded to controls. You can drop a hierarchy onto one of the prompt bars and it will resolve to a set of controls with cascading filters. The appropriate controls will be chosen based upon the cardinality of the participating categories.

In SAS Visual Analytics there is only one type of document and it is referred to as a Report. Whether you are working with Text or a Linear Regression all report objects are added to the pages within a report. All objects can participate in the richness of the various layouts supported within SAS Visual Analytics.

At the same time SAS Visual Analytics offers a more transient page that is referred to as Explore mode. With the click of a button on the object toolbar you can quickly see the data behind your objects. This is true for basic objects like a bar chart, but also for basic analytics like a correlation matrix or more advanced analytics like gradient boosting. More advanced objects will show supplemental information that helps describe the object.

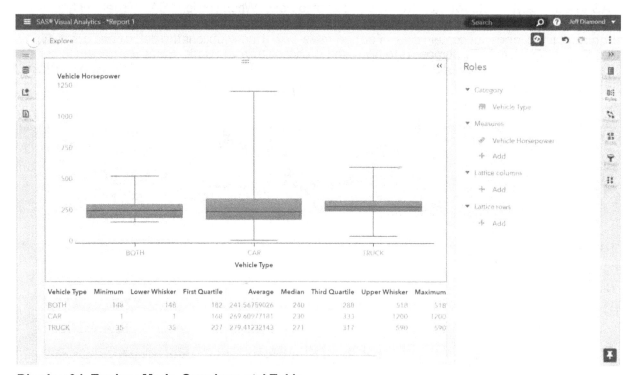

Display 31. Explore Mode, Supplemental Table

In Explore mode it's also easy to compare two or more objects. Regardless of where the objects might live in the report you can select or deselect objects via the Outline pane to see them, side-by-side, in Explore mode or hide them from view without deleting them from the report. You can even add new objects on this page by duplicating an existing object or adding new objects directly to the page. These new objects will automatically be added to your report even when you exit Explore mode.

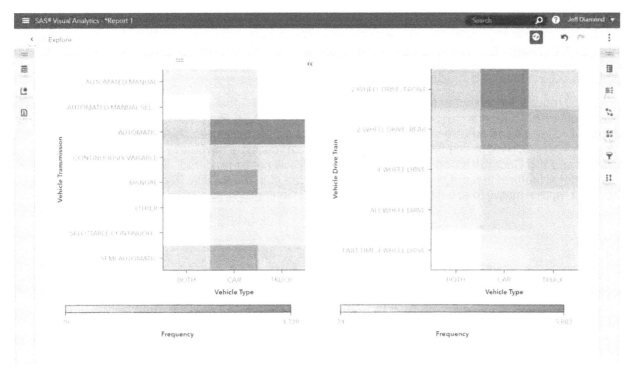

Display 42. Explore Mode, Comparison

There are many other benefits which are inherent when blending the best of all SAS Visual Analytics applications. Everything you build can be viewed on the Web or Mobile or in Office. All reports can be printed to PDF and the data for all objects can be exported.

The blending of data exploration, reporting and modeling into a single application will reduce confusion about which application to use. In addition, it will reduce the frustration of moving across tools with similar, but sometimes different interfaces. The sometimes hard to explain functional differences simply disappear.

MOVING FROM VERSION 7 TO VERSION 8

SAS recognizes the importance of making it easy for you to move from Version 7 to Version 8.

This starts with content. The format of SAS Visual Analytics reports remains unchanged. You can export all your reports to a package (.spk) and import them into your SAS Viya environment. As in the past you can use SAS® Management Console to create packages. In 8.1 SAS offers a well-documented command line interface (CLI) to import packages. A traditional user interface is planned for a later release. The import will bring all of your reports into your new environment. As in the past it will retain all images used by this report and all links between reports. The folder structure will be retained as well; however, the permissions on these folders will have to be reapplied. This is a known limitation and a problem we aim to resolve. Finally, while all reports can be promoted to the new environment you will not be able to promote your explorations until the upcoming 8.2 release. For the time being the explorations can be exported as a report in Version 7 and moved to Version 8. This will allow most, but not all, of the content in the exploration to be promoted.

In addition to moving your content you will also want to move your data. Because SAS Visual Analytics 8.1 is built atop SAS Viya you will need to move your data from LASR to CAS. First, it's useful to offer a little perspective about CAS. CAS is the next generation in memory server for SAS Viya. It can run all the SAS Visual Analytics operations that LASR supported. It offers key advantages as well. The most important is failover protection. Also, if data used by a report is not loaded it will automatically load it (Just-In-Time) when the report is loaded.

There are a few ways to move your data. One of the easiest and most common ways to move data from LASR to CAS is to import the data via SAS® Visual Data Builder or SAS Visual Analytics. You simply provide the credentials to your LASR server and choose the LASR tables you want to load into CAS. You can also load the data directly from a number of different formats including but not limited to SAS Data Sets, Excel, Hadoop, and Oracle.

After you move your content and data to SAS Visual Analytics 8.1 there are a couple of things to be aware of. First, all reports can be viewed immediately in the SAS® Report Viewer. With the exception of Stored Processes and custom report themes the reports should look and behave just as they did in Version 7. If you need to edit these reports there will be a few more caveats to be aware of. Custom graphs and KPI Grids will remain intact in the report, but will not be rendered. There are a small number of additional features that are not supported in 8.1, but are planned for 8.2. Please check with your account representative to see if these apply to your situation.

WHAT'S NEW

The application is written to work atop the SAS Viya platform. All interfaces are written in HTML5 instead of Flash. SAS Visual Analytics Designer, SAS Visual Analytics Explorer, and SAS Visual Statistics are merged into a single web application. A new offering, SAS Visual Data Mining and Machine Learning, is also integrated into the same web application. The interface is redesigned from the ground up to offer a very modern look and feel. These are the most significant enhancements for SAS Visual Analytics 8.1, but there are also a number of other important functional and usability enhancements.

There is a new type of object called Web Content. With this object you can integrate any HTML content that can be rendered in an iFrame. This includes video content. For sites that are running SAS 9 you can also use the URL for your SAS 9 Stored Process and integrate it directly in your 8.1 report.

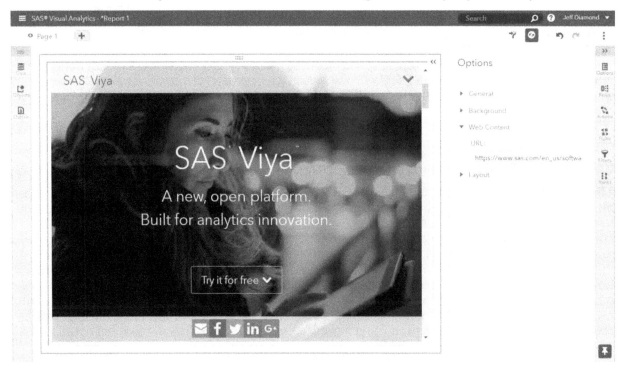

Display 53. Web Content

Have you always wanted cascading prompts in your report and page headers? SAS Visual Analytics 8.1 allows you filter and brush objects within these prompt bars.

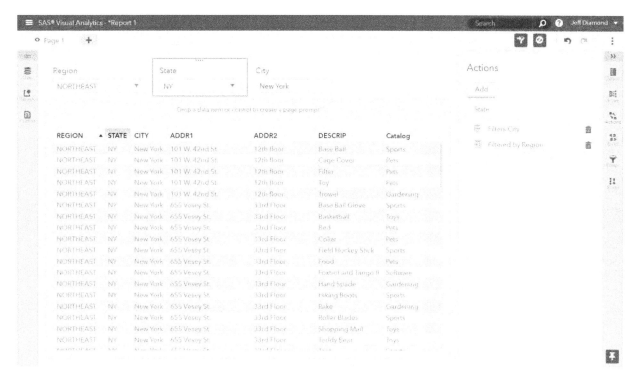

Display 64. Cascading Prompts

Your pie chart can easily be turned into a donut. The graph animations have been improved considerably.

Display 75. Pie Chart (Donut)

There are modern touches strewn throughout. The new report theme, Umstead, offers a new color palette and there is more padding around objects.

There is deeper integration with ESRI including Geo search and drive time analysis.

An inventive data cache has been added so that like queries will not make additional calls to the in memory server. This cache analyzes the security context and applies across users and reports. This can mean faster results and less load on your server.

The controls and text now support preferred sizing. This is important because it will make reports more portable across varying screen sizes. There will be significantly less empty space in your report (when moving to bigger screens) and fewer scrollbars (when moving to smaller screens).

If you are a user of precision layout you no longer need to make an entire page "precision" to take advantage of this feature. You can now make an individual container use precision layout and apply the extra effort only where you need it. This will make precision reports faster to author and potentially more portable across varying screen sizes.

Subtle delighters abound: heat map matrix, titles on prompt bars, URL images, and measures on lists, dropdowns, and text inputs. You can import data directly from your clipboard and drag data or images directly onto the interface for inclusion in the report. Titles can be edited inline and the interfaces for aggregated measures and calculated items were merged into one. Look around long enough and you'll find more!

We listened. You can now undo and redo all modifications to the report.

CONCLUSION

SAS Visual Analytics 8.1 has something exciting for everyone.

As you can see, SAS Visual Analytics has a fresh, new design that retains many familiar elements from previous release. It offers a clean, modern interface which is written using HTML5.

SAS Visual Analytics is a consolidation of SAS Visual Analytics Designer, SAS Visual Analytics Explorer, and SAS Visual Statistics. There is no more confusion of which tool is right for the job. There is no more frustration that one tool is missing a particular feature that is critical for you. This visual, interactive interface has also grown to include capabilities from new offerings like SAS Visual Data Mining and Machine Learning.

It is written for the SAS Viya environment and runs with the next generation in memory server. There are interfaces to help you move your data and reports from your SAS 9 environment to your SAS Viya environment.

Finally, there are many new features in version 8.1 and many more to come in the upcoming releases.

CONTACT INFORMATION

Your comments and questions are valued and encouraged. Contact the author at:

Jeff Diamond
100 SAS Campus Drive
Cary, NC 27513
SAS Institute Inc.
Jeff.Diamond@sas.com
http://www.sas.com

Paper 701-2017

The Future of Transpose: How SAS® Is Rebuilding Its Foundation by Making What Is Old New Again

Scott Mebust, SAS Institute Inc., Cary, NC

ABSTRACT

As computer technology advances, SAS® continually pursues opportunities to implement state-of-the-art systems that solve problems in data preparation and analysis faster and more efficiently. In this pursuit, we have extended the TRANSPOSE procedure to operate in a distributed fashion within both Teradata and Hadoop, using dynamically generated DS2 executed by the SAS® Embedded Process and within SAS® Viya™, using its native transpose action. With its new ability to work within these environments, PROC TRANSPOSE provides you with access to its parallel processing power and produces results that are compatible with your existing SAS programs.

INTRODUCTION

In a continuation of efforts to improve performance, process larger amounts of data, and take advantage of existing customer hardware and third-party software, SAS has enhanced the TRANSPOSE procedure to run in a distributed fashion within massively parallel processing (MPP) environments. These environments include the Teradata relational MPP database management system (DBMS), commodity computer clusters running Apache Hadoop, and SAS Cloud Analytic Services (CAS). CAS is a part of SAS Viya — the new and modern platform on which we are building the next generation of SAS analytics.

Operation within the Teradata DBMS and Hadoop, both known as in-database operation, is accomplished through the generation of DS2 program code submitted to the SAS Embedded Process (EP) for execution. Operation inside SAS Cloud Analytic Services, referred to here as in-CAS operation, is accomplished through a simple client request by PROC TRANSPOSE to invoke the new CAS transpose action on the CAS server. An understanding of the details of in-database transposition can provide you with an introduction to coding custom DS2 for in-database execution with the SAS® In-Database Code Accelerator. Understanding in-CAS operation can provide exposure to coding actions for execution by CAS. The DS2 generated for in-database operation can be examined in the SAS log and used to produce a stand-alone accelerated DS2 program that you can modify and extend. Likewise, the transpose action code generated for in-CAS operation can be examined and submitted to a CAS server, independently of PROC TRANSPOSE, using various clients and languages.

Even though the DBMS and CAS systems are very different from the traditional MultiVendor Architecture (MVA) system in which PROC TRANSPOSE usually runs, we have made great effort to ensure that in-database and in-CAS operation produce results that are compatible with the traditional system. If you've used PROC TRANSPOSE, then use of these new operational capabilities and their results should be familiar to you.

We encourage you to provide feedback on these new capabilities of PROC TRANSPOSE and on the new CAS transpose action. Your suggestions can help guide code development and make these tools more useful to you. One change that we are making in an upcoming release of SAS is the ability for the TRANSPOSE procedure to directly produce a stand-alone DS2 program that you can readily study and change. We hope that you find this change useful for exploration of DS2 and the In-Database Code Accelerator.

REQUIREMENTS

To take advantage of the new capabilities of PROC TRANSPOSE to run in-database with Teradata, when using Base SAS®, you need licenses for the SAS/ACCESS® Interface to Teradata, as well as SAS® In-Database Code Accelerator for Teradata. Similarly, for in-database operation on Hadoop, you need licenses for the SAS/ACCESS® Interface to Hadoop, as well as SAS® In-Database Code Accelerator for Hadoop. For operation in SAS Cloud Analytic Services, you need a license for SAS Viya 3.1 or a later release.

For the TRANSPOSE procedure to operate in-database, its input data set must be read from the DBMS and the results must be written to the DBMS. Likewise, for the TRANSPOSE procedure to operate in-CAS, it is necessary that the input resides in the server and the output data set is directed to the server. Other conditions, stated in sections below detailing the in-database and in-CAS examples, are also necessary for such operation. For SAS Viya, the transpose action operates only on input tables that are available in the CAS server and writes results to output tables in the same server.

GENERAL INTERNAL OPERATION

Transposition, as performed by SAS, is a dynamic transformation of an input data set, producing an output data set that is dependent not only on the transposition specification (the statements, variable lists, options, parameters, etc., that are coded by the user), but also on the characteristics of the variables to be transposed and the values of those variables within the input data. In particular, the types of variables to be transposed determine the types of the output variables. This determination is made with a type promotion scheme in which mixed input variable types result in an output variable type that is capable of representing the full range and precision of input values. The simplest example of this is that the transposition of both a numeric variable and a character variable results in character output variables. It is the transposition's dependence on the values of the input data, though, that makes it dynamic, not just statically defined by the transposition specification, and relieves the user from having to thoroughly know the input data prior to the transposition. A user does not have to specify an explicit list of variables to be created in the output data set or stipulate how values from input rows are assigned to those variables.

In the traditional MVA implementation of PROC TRANSPOSE, the in-database implementation, and the CAS transpose action implementation, the general process of transposition works similarly. All three implementations perform two read passes over the input data. The shape and characteristics of the output data set (the number of variables and their names) are determined during the first pass, while the actual transposition occurs during the second pass.

A SIMPLE TEST CASE

To demonstrate and focus on the details of in-database execution, in-CAS execution, and direct execution of the CAS transpose action, we transpose a very simple data set. The data set is a theoretical register or log of manufactured item measurements taken for quality control purposes, with three recorded values for each of two measurements within each batch:

```
data register;
  length property $ 20;
  input batch property value1 value2 value3;
  cards;
  1000 length    86.1 86.0 86.1
  1000 width     55.2 55.1 55.0
  1001 length    84.3 84.5 84.4
  1001 width     57.3 57.4 57.4
  ;
run;
```

Table 1 Shows the data to be transposed

Obs	batch	property	value1	value2	value3
1	1000	length	86.1	86.0	86.1
2	1000	width	55.2	55.1	55.0
3	1001	length	84.3	84.5	84.4
4	1001	width	57.3	57.4	57.4

Table 1: Register data set

For the sake of preparation or analysis, we transpose this data so that the two measurements (length and width) are each represented by one variable in the transposed data set:

```
proc transpose data=register out=measurements;
 by batch;
 id property;
 var value1-value3;
run;
```

Table 2 Shows the data after transposition

Obs	batch	_NAME_	length	width
1	1000	value1	86.1	55.2
2	1000	value2	86.0	55.1
3	1000	value3	86.1	55.0
4	1001	value1	84.3	57.3
5	1001	value2	84.5	57.4
6	1001	value3	84.4	57.4

Table 2: Measurements data set

IN-DATABASE EXAMPLE

To operate within a DBMS or Hadoop, we must start with the data set residing in the remote system, so we first place it there using a DATA step. For this example, the GRIDLIB library has been established using a SAS/ACCESS engine (either to Teradata or to Hadoop). To run in-database, even though in-database transposition is largely performed by running DS2 code, it is also necessary that the system SQLGENERATION option is properly set. The SQLGENERATION option remains relevant because in-database operation is traditionally controlled with this option and the same underlying infrastructure, as well as some generated SQL, is used to run the DS2. Use of the MSGLEVEL and SQL_IP_TRACE options provide more feedback in the SAS log regarding the process and internal operations. Note that both the DATA= and OUT= options reference data sets in the GRIDLIB library. Furthermore, note the use of the BY statement, the ID statement, the INDB=YES option setting, and the LET option. These are all required for in-database operation:

```
data gridlib.register;
 set register;
run;

options sqlgeneration=dbms;
options msglevel=i;
options sql_ip_trace=source;

proc transpose
    data=gridlib.register
    out=gridlib.measurements
    INDB=YES
    LET;
 by batch;
 id property;
 var value1-value3;
run;
```

The specification of at least one BY variable in a BY statement is required to define groups of observations that are transposed in parallel. One or more ID variables are required to define assignment of input rows to output columns and the names of those output columns. This assignment is made by associating a particular output column with the column name that was formed from the formatted values of the ID variables of an input observation. Without an ID variable, the assignment of values from input observations to output variables would be nondeterministic, with such assignments likely varying among BY groups, because of the nondeterminism inherent in MPP DBMSs and similar parallel processing systems. Such nondeterministic assignments would produce output that is difficult to validate and replicate. Because of this, we limit transpositions to ones requiring a mapping between input rows and output columns defined by one or more ID variables.

Finally, the LET option is required because PROC TRANSPOSE does not detect data loss, caused by more than one input observation within a BY group being transposed to a single output variable, during in-database operation. The TRANSPOSE procedure, when running in its traditional manner, stops with an error message during its first pass if the ID variables from two or more input observations within a BY group produce the same output variable name. The error means that two or more input observations within the group are assigned to the same output variable and only the values from the last transposed observation are output if execution continues. However, for efficiency of processing in the first pass, PROC TRANSPOSE does not attempt to detect this situation when running in-database. To protect you from data loss, PROC TRANSPOSE will not run in-database unless the LET option is specified. The LET option allows (or lets) this data loss to occur. Furthermore, because data loss is not detected, PROC TRANSPOSE does not issue any warning messages if data loss does occur when running in-database. Use the LET option to allow in-database operation if you understand your data and are certain that the specified ID variables ensure only one input observation is assigned to any one output variable or if you accept the possibility of data loss due to many-to-one assignments.

IN-DATABASE INTERNAL OPERATION

Two separate DS2 programs are generated and executed within the EP, one for each pass over the input data. The first program determines the shape of the output transposition by discovering the set of unique output column names generated from the ID variable values for each observation of the input data set. This DS2 program, indicated in the SAS log as the SHAPE QUERY, achieves a high degree of parallelism by performing the determination and discovery within its thread program using a sequential scan, with each thread reading a portion of data. The sets of column names generated by each thread are aggregated by a second stage data program that performs the same task. The DS2 code for this program is revealed by setting the SQL_IP_TRACE system option to SOURCE or ALL. The code for the above test case, when formatted, looks like this:

```
data sasep.out;

  retain "property" "_NAME_" ;
  declare double TPS_RC;
  declare package hash TPS_HASH();
  declare package hiter TPS_HITER('TPS_HASH');
  declare package tpsn TPS_TPSN('','','','V7');
  declare nchar(32) "_NAME_";
  keep "property" ;

  method init();
    TPS_HASH.defineKey('"_NAME_"');
    TPS_HASH.defineData('"_NAME_"');
    TPS_HASH.defineData('"property"');
    TPS_HASH.defineDone();
  end;

  method run();
    declare char(20) TPS_RAWVAL1;
```

```
  set sasep.in;
  if not ( missing( "property" )  );

  TPS_TPSN.reset();
  TPS_TPSN.build(["property"],'$',20,0);
  TPS_TPSN.finalize();

  "_NAME_" = TPS_TPSN.copyname();

  TPS_RAWVAL1 = "property";
  TPS_RC = TPS_HASH.find();
  if ( TPS_RC = 0 )
  then
    do;
      if ( TPS_RAWVAL1 < "property" )
      then "property" = TPS_RAWVAL1;
      TPS_RC = TPS_HASH.replace();
    end;
  else
    do;
      TPS_RC = TPS_HASH.add();
    end;
  end;

  method term();
    TPS_RC = TPS_HITER.first();
    do while ( TPS_RC = 0 );
      output;
      TPS_RC = TPS_HITER.next();
    end;
  end;

enddata;
```

This first program creates variable names using a DS2 package called TPSN, the sole purpose of which is to form output variable names from the formatted values of one or more ID variables that conform to SAS variable naming conventions, as determined by the VALIDVARNAME system option. The TPSN package is not documented and is for internal use by PROC TRANSPOSE and related code only; however, you can write your own DS2 package that performs a similar function, if you want to implement a similar transformation or use a different method for associating input observations to output variables. For every input observation, an output variable name is created and inserted into a Hash object, which maintains the list of unique names, along with representative raw values of the ID variables.

Note that, because this program is in a format that is suitable for execution by the EP, it is not directly executable as a stand-alone DS2. However, it can be transformed into a stand-alone program. Although the listed code appears to be a data program, it serves as both the DS2 thread program and second-stage aggregation data program. To transform this code into a stand-alone DS2 program, use the program structure below and follow the instructions within the comments:

```
proc ds2 indb=yes;
  thread th_pgm / overwrite=yes;

    /***********************************************
    1. Insert code between DATA and ENDDATA here.
    2. Replace SASEP.IN with input data set name.
    ***********************************************/
```

5

```
    endthread;
    run;

    /*********************************************************
       1. Insert code, from DATA to ENDDATA inclusive, here.
       2. Replace SASEP.OUT with temporary data set name
       3. Declare a thread th_pgm M at top of data program
       4. Replace SET SASEP.IN with SET FROM M
       *********************************************************/
  run;
quit;
```

The resulting stand-alone program is:

```
proc ds2 indb=yes;

  thread th_pgm / overwrite=yes;

    retain "property" "_NAME_" ;
    declare double TPS_RC;
    declare package hash TPS_HASH();
    declare package hiter TPS_HITER('TPS_HASH');
    declare package tpsn TPS_TPSN('','','','V7');
    declare nchar(32) "_NAME_";
    keep "property" ;

    method init();
      TPS_HASH.defineKey('"_NAME_"');
      TPS_HASH.defineData('"_NAME_"');
      TPS_HASH.defineData('"property"');
      TPS_HASH.defineDone();
    end;

    method run();
      declare char(20) TPS_RAWVAL1;

      set gridlib.register;
      if not ( missing( "property" )  );

      TPS_TPSN.reset();
      TPS_TPSN.build(["property"],'$',20,0);
      TPS_TPSN.finalize();

      "_NAME_" = TPS_TPSN.copyname();

      TPS_RAWVAL1 = "property";
      TPS_RC = TPS_HASH.find();
      if ( TPS_RC = 0 )
      then
        do;
          if ( TPS_RAWVAL1 < "property" )
          then "property" = TPS_RAWVAL1;
          TPS_RC = TPS_HASH.replace();
        end;
      else
        do;
```

6

```
        TPS_RC = TPS_HASH.add();
      end;
  end;

  method term();
    TPS_RC = TPS_HITER.first();
    do while ( TPS_RC = 0 );
      output;
      TPS_RC = TPS_HITER.next();
    end;
  end;

endthread;
run;

data gridlib.metadata;

  declare thread th_pgm m;

  retain "property" "_NAME_" ;
  declare double TPS_RC;
  declare package hash TPS_HASH();
  declare package hiter TPS_HITER('TPS_HASH');
  declare package tpsn TPS_TPSN('','','','V7');
  declare nchar(32) "_NAME_";
  keep "property" ;

  method init();
    TPS_HASH.defineKey('"_NAME_"');
    TPS_HASH.defineData('"_NAME_"');
    TPS_HASH.defineData('"property"');
    TPS_HASH.defineDone();
  end;

  method run();
    declare char(20) TPS_RAWVAL1;

    set from m;
    if not ( missing( "property" )  );

    TPS_TPSN.reset();
    TPS_TPSN.build(["property"],'$',20,0);
    TPS_TPSN.finalize();

    "_NAME_" = TPS_TPSN.copyname();

    TPS_RAWVAL1 = "property";
    TPS_RC = TPS_HASH.find();
    if ( TPS_RC = 0 )
    then
      do;
        if ( TPS_RAWVAL1 < "property" )
        then "property" = TPS_RAWVAL1;
        TPS_RC = TPS_HASH.replace();
      end;
    else
      do;
```

```
            TPS_RC = TPS_HASH.add();
          end;
      end;

    method term();
      TPS_RC = TPS_HITER.first();
      do while ( TPS_RC = 0 );
        output;
        TPS_RC = TPS_HITER.next();
      end;
    end;

  enddata;
  run;
quit;
```

You can run this first program within the local SAS session if you change INDB=NO. As is, with INDB=YES, the code runs within the EP using DS2 code acceleration. In this case, you should see the following notes in the SAS log:

```
NOTE: Running THREAD program in-database
NOTE: Running DATA program in-database
```

The second program, generated with the aid of the output variable metadata that was returned from the execution of the first program, actually performs the transposition. This DS2 program, indicated in the SAS log as the TRANSPOSE QUERY, achieves parallelism through the transposition of independent BY groups. BY-group processing, triggered by the presence of the BY statement within a thread program, causes the underlying system (Teradata or Hadoop) to shuffle and order the observations so that they are grouped before processing. For Teradata, this involves the use of the BY variables in HASH BY and ORDER BY clauses on the SELECT statement of the SQL query that provides data to the EP. For Hadoop, the BY variables are used as the Map/Reduce keys, which results in a shuffle and sort.

Partitioning of the data can be costly, in terms of computational resources. Pre-partitioning of the input tables within those systems, in preparation for such group processing, can eliminate the need to shuffle the data when running the transposition. You might choose to pre-partition the input if partitioned access is required for more than one purpose. For a more detailed description of how DS2 code can be accelerated within the EP, see the recommended reading material listed at the end of this paper. Again, the DS2 code for this program can be revealed by setting the SQL_IP_TRACE system option to SOURCE or ALL. The formatted code for the above test case is:

```
data sasep.out;
  retain "batch" "_NAME_" "_LABEL_" ;
  retain "width" "length" ;
  declare package hash TPS_HASH();
  declare package tpsn TPS_TPSN('','','','V7');
  declare integer TPS_COL;
  declare nchar(32) "_NAME_" having label 'NAME OF FORMER VARIABLE';
  declare nchar(32) TPS_INVNAM[ 3 ];
  declare nchar(40) "_LABEL_";
  declare nchar(40) TPS_INVLAB[ 3 ];
  vararray double TPS_INVARS[ 3 ] "value1" "value2" "value3" ;
  vararray double TPS_OUTVARS[ 2 ] "width" "length" ;
  declare double TPS_TPOSETMP[ 3, 2 ];
  keep "batch" "_NAME_" "_LABEL_" "width" "length" ;

  method init();
    TPS_HASH.defineKey('"_NAME_"');
```

```
    TPS_HASH.defineData('"_NAME_"');
    TPS_HASH.defineData('"TPS_COL"');
    TPS_HASH.defineDone();

    "_NAME_" = 'width';
    TPS_COL = 1;
    TPS_HASH.add();

    "_NAME_" = 'length';
    TPS_COL = 2;
    TPS_HASH.add();

    TPS_INVNAM := ( 'value1' 'value2' 'value3'  );
    TPS_INVLAB := ( 'value1' 'value2' 'value3'  );
end;

method run();
  declare integer TPS_ROW;
  declare double TPS_RC;
  set sasep.in ;
  by "batch" ;
  if not ( missing( "property" )  )
  then
    do;
      TPS_TPSN.reset();
      TPS_TPSN.build(["property"],'$',20,0);
      TPS_TPSN.finalize();
      "_NAME_" = TPS_TPSN.copyname();

      TPS_RC = TPS_HASH.find();
      if ( TPS_RC )
      then
        do;
          put 'ERROR: Unexpected error, _NAME_ not found.';
          stop;
        end;

      do TPS_ROW = 1 to 3;
        TPS_TPOSETMP[ TPS_ROW, TPS_COL ] = TPS_INVARS[ TPS_ROW ];
      end;
    end;

  if last."batch"
  then
    do;
      do TPS_ROW = 1 to 3;
        "_NAME_" = TPS_INVNAM[ TPS_ROW ];
        "_LABEL_" = TPS_INVLAB[ TPS_ROW ];
        do TPS_COL = 1 to 2 ;
          TPS_OUTVARS[ TPS_COL ] = TPS_TPOSETMP[ TPS_ROW, TPS_COL ];
        end;
        output;
      end;
      TPS_TPOSETMP := ( 3 * ( 2 * NULL ) );
    end;
end;
```

```
    method term();
  end;
enddata;
```

Although the generated code is enclosed in a DATA ... ENDDATA block, this code is really the DS2 thread program, which executes independently, but in parallel, with each thread processing one or more BY groups. The DS2 code begins with declarations of variables, both those used to accomplish the transposition, but not included in the output, and those results of the transposition kept for the output. The type of variable elements in the transposition matrix, TPS_TPOSETMP, as well as the types of the output variables WIDTH and LENGTH, are determined by the type of those input variables listed on the VAR statement. In this case, the variables VALUE1, VALUE2, and VALUE3 are all of type double, thus the transposition matrix and output variables are doubles as well. The output type is simple to determine for this example, but the type of promotion scheme used to determine the output variable type supports the full complement of DS2 variable types. These declarations are followed by the initialization of a Hash Object with key/value pairs that map names produced by the formatted values of ID variables, for each observation to a corresponding column in the transposition matrix. The keys of the key/value pairs used to initialize the Hash Object are the output variable names determined during the first pass from the execution of the first DS2 program.

The code then processes a group of observations by reading each observation of the group, transposing the values for the variables of interest of that observation into a column of the transposition matrix. The ordinal of the column into which the observation is transposed is identified by searching the Hash Object for the name produced from the ID variable values of that observation. After all observations of a group are processed in this way, the transposition is completed by outputting each row of the transposition matrix. After output is complete, the transposition matrix is cleared so that another observation group can be processed.

This code will not execute as a stand-alone DS2 program, because it is generated to be executed by the EP. For the purposes of learning, modifying, or extending the code, you can easily transform the code into a stand-alone DS2 program by using the program structure below and following the instructions within the comments:

```
proc ds2 indb=yes;

  thread th_pgm / overwrite=yes;

    /********************************************************
       1. Insert code between DATA and ENDDATA here.
       2. Replace SASEP.IN with input data set name.
       ******************************************************/

  endthread;
  run;


  /********************************************************
     1. Create a new data program here that does nothing
        but declares and sets from a thread.
     2. Direct output of the data program to a data set
        on the grid.

     For example:
     ******************************************************/

  data LIBNAME.DATASETNAME(overwrite=yes);

    declare thread th_pgm m;
```

```
    method run();
     set from m;
    end;

  enddata;
  run;

quit;
```

Arranged this way, with the data program doing nothing but invoking the thread program, the threads perform parallel output of the transposed data.

The resulting stand-alone program for the above test case is:

```
proc ds2 indb=yes;

  thread th_pgm / overwrite=yes;

    retain "batch" "_NAME_" "_LABEL_" ;
    retain "width" "length" ;
    declare package hash TPS_HASH();
    declare package tpsn TPS_TPSN('','','','V7');
    declare integer TPS_COL;
    declare nchar(32) "_NAME_" having label 'NAME OF FORMER VARIABLE';
    declare nchar(32) TPS_INVNAM[ 3 ];
    declare nchar(40) "_LABEL_";
    declare nchar(40) TPS_INVLAB[ 3 ];
    vararray double TPS_INVARS[ 3 ] "value1" "value2" "value3" ;
    vararray double TPS_OUTVARS[ 2 ] "width" "length" ;
    declare double TPS_TPOSETMP[ 3, 2 ];
    keep "batch" "_NAME_" "_LABEL_" "width" "length" ;

    method init();
      TPS_HASH.defineKey('"_NAME_"');
      TPS_HASH.defineData('"_NAME_"');
      TPS_HASH.defineData('"TPS_COL"');
      TPS_HASH.defineDone();

      "_NAME_" = 'width';
      TPS_COL = 1;
      TPS_HASH.add();

      "_NAME_" = 'length';
      TPS_COL = 2;
      TPS_HASH.add();

      TPS_INVNAM := ( 'value1' 'value2' 'value3'  );
      TPS_INVLAB := ( 'value1' 'value2' 'value3'  );
    end;

    method run();
      declare integer TPS_ROW;
      declare double TPS_RC;
      set gridlib.register;
      by "batch" ;
      if not ( missing( "property" )  )
      then
```

11

```
    do;
       TPS_TPSN.reset();
       TPS_TPSN.build(["property"],'$',20,0);
       TPS_TPSN.finalize();
       "_NAME_" = TPS_TPSN.copyname();

       TPS_RC = TPS_HASH.find();
       if ( TPS_RC )
       then
          do;
             put 'ERROR: Unexpected error, _NAME_ not found.';
             stop;
          end;

       do TPS_ROW = 1 to 3;
          TPS_TPOSETMP[ TPS_ROW, TPS_COL ] =
             TPS_INVARS[ TPS_ROW ];
       end;
    end;

  if last."batch"
  then
     do;
        do TPS_ROW = 1 to 3;
           "_NAME_" = TPS_INVNAM[ TPS_ROW ];
           "_LABEL_" = TPS_INVLAB[ TPS_ROW ];
           do TPS_COL = 1 to 2 ;
              TPS_OUTVARS[ TPS_COL ] =
                 TPS_TPOSETMP[ TPS_ROW, TPS_COL ];
           end;
           output;
        end;
        TPS_TPOSETMP := ( 3 * ( 2 * NULL ) );
     end;
end;

method term();
end;

endthread;

run;

data gridlib.measurements(overwrite=yes);

  declare thread th_pgm m;
  method run();
   set from m;
  end;

enddata;

run;

quit;
```

Like the stand-alone DS2 program for the first-pass, you can run this program within the local SAS session if you change INDB=NO. With INDB=YES, the code runs within the EP, using DS2 code acceleration. When run within the EP, you should see the following notes in the SAS log:

```
NOTE: Running THREAD program in-database
NOTE: Running DATA program in-database
```

IN-CAS EXAMPLE

To operate within the CAS server, we must also start with the data set residing in the server. For this example, having established a SASCAS1 libref using the SAS/ACCESS engine to CAS, we copy the data from the WORK library to the server using a DATA step. Unlike in-database operation, no DS2 code is generated and no EP is involved. Instead, PROC TRANSPOSE on the SAS client simply requests that the CAS transpose action is invoked on its behalf within the CAS server. Other than both the DATA= and OUT= options referencing data sets in the SASCAS1 library, the only requirement here for in-CAS operation is the use of an ID statement and the specification of one or more ID variables to determine the transposition:

```
data sascas1.register;
  set register;
run;

proc print data=sascas1.register;
  var batch property value1-value3;
run;

options msglevel=i;

proc transpose
    data=sascas1.register
    out=sascas1.measurements;
  by batch;
  id property;
  var value1-value3;
run;
```

While not strictly required, using a BY statement with the specification of one or more BY variables is suggested because, like in-database operation, parallelism in the transposition is achieved through the distribution of different BY groups across the computing nodes in the system and the simultaneous processing of BY groups on those nodes. A transposition with no BY statement implies a single BY group and the processing of all data on a single node.

The LET option is not required for in-CAS operation, because the underlying CAS transpose action detects during the first pass when the values of two or more observations within an input group are assigned to a single output variable. If the LET option has not been specified, like traditional PROC TRANSPOSE, the action stops with an error when data loss is detected. If you encounter such an error, you can use the LET option to ignore the data loss and allow the transposition to complete.

IN-CAS INTERNAL OPERATION

For execution within the CAS server, the TRANSPOSE procedure on the SAS client issues a request to the server to run the CAS transpose action. That request can be revealed by recalling the history of client and server interactions, using the HISTORY statement with the CAS procedure:

```
proc cas;
  session sascas1;
  run;
```

```
      history verbose first=-4 last=-4;
    run;
  quit;
```

The FIRST and LAST options are used to extract the specific interaction containing the transpose action request. After requesting the history, the output of the action code can be extracted from the SAS log. For this test case, that action code is:

```
action transpose.transpose /
    table={name='REGISTER', groupBy={{name='batch'}}},
    id={'property'},
    casOut={name='MEASUREMENTS', replace=true},
    validVarName='v7',
    transpose={'value1', 'value2', 'value3'};
```

While the syntax of the transpose action is obviously different from that of the TRANSPOSE procedure, the meaning of the action parameters is likely reasonably clear, because most parameters can be directly related to procedure statements and options. The action's TABLE parameter corresponds to the DATA option of the TRANSPOSE procedure statement. Likewise, the CASOUT parameter corresponds to the OUT option of the procedure statement. The ID parameter is the equivalent of the procedure's ID statement. The GROUPBY parameter, a sub-parameter of the action's TABLE parameter, contains the list of variables that appear on the BY statement. The VALIDVARNAME parameter is set for compatibility with the client, based on the SAS client setting of the VALIDVARNAME system option. Finally, the action's transpose parameter takes the list of variables to be transposed that appear on the VAR statement. Operation of the transpose action within CAS is described below.

INVOKING TRANSPOSE ACTION DIRECTLY

This action code, revealed in the SAS log by the CAS procedure's HISTORY statement and presented in the CAS language, can be used directly within PROC CAS. Running PROC TRANSPOSE is familiar to SAS programmers and integrates neatly into standard SAS code. Running the action code directly from PROC CAS allows expression of a work and data flow, using the power of the new CAS language:

```
proc cas;
  session sascas1;
  run;

  loadactionset "transpose";
  run;

  action transpose.transpose /
    table={name='REGISTER', groupBy={{name='batch'}}},
    id={'property'},
    casOut={name='MEASUREMENTS', replace=true},
    validVarName='v7',
    transpose={'value1', 'value2', 'value3'};
  run;
quit;
```

In addition to the CAS language, all CAS actions can be invoked using other CAS client languages, such as Lua and Python, as well as through a web service using HTTP with a REST API*.

*Using the Hypertext Transfer Protocol (HTTP) with a Representational State Transfer (REST) application programming Interface (API).

TRANSPOSE ACTION INTERNAL OPERATION

An action in CAS is roughly the equivalent of a procedure in the traditional SAS system. The transpose action is a native part of CAS and does not generate any intermediate code for execution. Because it is coded at a lower level and can open its input table in two-pass mode, it first requests that the input table be partitioned according to the GROUPBY variables and then performs two passes: the first to determine the shape of the output table and the second to perform the transposition. Making two passes over the grouped data allows the action to check for potential data loss, like traditional PROC TRANSPOSE does. If data loss is detected and the LET option is not specified, the action issues one or more error messages and stops execution. If the LET option is specified and data loss is detected, the action issues one or more warning messages, but continues execution.

Similar to traditional and in-database operation, the action determines the shape and characteristics of the output table during its first pass over the input. It ascertains the type of output variables based on the input variables specified for transposition and supports the new CAS variable types. Like the TRANSPOSE procedure, if no variables are specified for transposition, then all double-precision, floating-point variables that are not used for other purposes (as ID or GROUPBY variable, for instance) are transposed.

COMPATIBILITY

With any changes that SAS makes in new releases of software in use by customers, whether adding new features to existing procedures or adding whole new methods of operation, we take great care to maintain compatibility with the behavior and results to which customers are accustomed. While it is not always possible to build upon the existing system and maintain 100% compatibility with prior releases, it is certainly the goal for which we strive. The creation of the TRANSPOSE procedure's new in-database and in-CAS modes of operation are no exception. We have tried to ensure that the results you obtain from PROC TRANSPOSE and the new CAS transpose action are consistent with traditional results that are produced by the SAS system. For these new capabilities, we have paid particular attention to the treatment of missing values, characteristics of output data sets, formatting of variables in output, and use of formats in the formation of variables names. In doing so, we hope to provide new power and performance, while preserving your investment in our software.

FUTURE DIRECTIONS

We encourage you to try the new capabilities of PROC TRANSPOSE to perform its work in remote systems, such as Teradata and Hadoop, using in-database operation and SAS Viya using in-CAS operation. We hope that you find the DS2 code generated for in-database operation useful for building upon or simply learning about DS2 and the SAS In-Database Code Accelerator. We also encourage you to investigate the new SAS Viya platform as we introduce it. We welcome feedback regarding the changes in PROC TRANSPOSE, as well as the introduction of the CAS transpose action. In addition to continued focus on efficiency, quality, and compatibility of this new software, we intend to make it easier to run PROC TRANSPOSE jobs in-database and to produce stand-alone DS2 programs from the generated code used for in-database operation. To produce a stand-alone program, we envision a new procedure option that writes the DS2 code to a text file.

RECOMMENDED READING

Secosky, Jason, et al. 2014. "Parallel Data Preparation with the DS2 Programming Language." *Proceedings of the SAS Global Forum 2014 Conference*. Cary, NC: SAS Institute Inc. Available at http://support.sas.com/resources/papers/proceedings14/SAS329-2014.pdf.

Ghazaleh, David. 2016. "Exploring SAS® Embedded Process Technologies on Hadoop®." *Proceedings of the SAS Global Forum 2016 Conference*. Cary, NC: SAS Institute Inc. Available at http://support.sas.com/resources/papers/proceedings16/SAS5060-2016.pdf.

De Capite, Donna. 2014. "Techniques in Processing Data on Hadoop®." *Proceedings of the SAS Global Forum 2014 Conference*. Cary, NC: SAS Institute Inc. Available at https://support.sas.com/resources/papers/proceedings14/SAS033-2014.pdf

Ray, Robert, et al. 2016. "Data Analysis with User-Written DS2 Packages." *Proceedings of the SAS Global Forum 2016 Conference*. Cary, NC: SAS Institute Inc. Available at http://support.sas.com/resources/papers/proceedings16/SAS6462-2016.pdf

Secosky, Jason, et al. 2007. "Getting Started with the DATA Step Hash Object." *Proceedings of the SAS Global Forum 2007 Conference*. Cary, NC: SAS Institute Inc. Available at http://www2.sas.com/proceedings/forum2007/271-2007.pdf

SAS Institute Inc. 2015. *SAS 9.4 In-Database Products, User's Guide, 5th ed.* Cary, NC: SAS Institute Inc. Available at https://support.sas.com/documentation/cdl/en/indbug/68170/PDF/default/indbug.pdf

SAS Institute Inc. 2016. *SAS 9.4 DS2 Language Reference, 6th ed.* Cary, NC: SAS Institute Inc. Available at

http://support.sas.com/documentation/cdl/en/ds2ref/69739/PDF/default/ds2ref.pdf

SAS Institute Inc. 2016. *Base SAS 9.4 Procedures Guide, 6th ed.* Cary, NC: SAS Institute Inc. Available at

http://support.sas.com/documentation/cdl/en/proc/69850/PDF/default/proc.pdf

ACKNOWLEDGMENTS

Thanks to all those who reviewed this paper and provided feedback on its content. In particular, thanks to Robert Ray, Laura Gold, Mark Freskos, and John West.

CONTACT INFORMATION

Your comments and questions are valued and encouraged. Contact the author at:

Scott Mebust
100 SAS Campus Drive
Cary, NC 27513
SAS Insitute Inc.
Scott.Mebust@sas.com
http://www.sas.com

Paper SAS668-2017

I Am Multilingual: A Comparison of the Python, Java, Lua, and REST Interfaces to SAS® Viya™

Xiangxiang Meng and Kevin D Smith, SAS Institute Inc.

ABSTRACT

The openness of SAS® Viya™, the new cloud analytic platform centered around SAS® Cloud Analytic Services (CAS), emphasizes a unified experience for data scientists. You can now execute the analytic capabilities of SAS® from different programming languages including Python, Java, and Lua, as well as use a RESTful endpoint to execute CAS actions directly. This paper provides an introduction to these programming language interfaces. For each language, we illustrate how the API is surfaced from the CAS server, the types of data that you can upload to a CAS server, and the result tables that are returned. This paper also provides a comprehensive comparison of using these programming languages to build a common analytical process, including connecting to a CAS server; exploring, manipulating, and visualizing data; and building statistical and machine learning models.

INTRODUCTION

This paper provides an introduction to the different programming interfaces to SAS® Cloud Analytic Services (CAS). CAS is the central analytic environment for SAS® Viya™, which enables a user to submit and execute the same analytic actions from different programming languages or SAS applications. Besides CAS-enabled SAS® procedures, CAS provides interfaces for programming languages such as Python, Java, and Lua. You can also submit actions over the HTTP and HTTPS protocols in other languages using the REST API that is surfaced by CAS.

We compare these interfaces and illustrate how to connect to the CAS server, submit CAS actions, and work with the results returned by CAS actions in Python, Lua, and Java. We then provide examples on data summarization, data exploration, and building analytic models. Finally, we cover some examples of how to use the REST interface to submit CAS actions.

IMPORTING CLIENT SIDE PACKAGES

In this paper, we assume you already have a running CAS server and have some data loaded to the CAS server. For each client (Python, Lua, or Java), you need to import the client side package provided by SAS. These are available for download from support.sas.com. In Python or Lua, This interface is called **SWAT** (Scripting Wrapper for Analytics Transfer). SWAT is a SAS architecture that enables you to interact with a CAS server from different scripting languages such as Python and Lua. The code below demonstrates how to load the SWAT package in Python and Lua.

```
Python
In [1]: import swat
```

```
Lua
> swat = require 'swat'
```

The Java **CAS Client** provides access to CAS using socket protocols. Unlike the scripting interfaces, the CAS Client is not based on the SWAT architecture; it is pure Java. You can import the Java classes individually:

```
Java
import com.sas.cas.CASActionResults;
import com.sas.cas.CASClient;
import com.sas.cas.CASClientInterface;
import com.sas.cas.CASValue;
```

Alternatively, you can load all classes in com.sas.cas:

```Java
import com.sas.cas.*;
```

CONNECTING TO CAS

In this paper, we assume that a CAS server is running. To connect to a CAS server, you need to know the host name or the IP address of the server, and the port number. You must have an authenticated user account. In Python and Lua, you can use the **CAS** object to set up a new connection.

```Python
In [2]: conn = swat.CAS('cas.mycompany.com', 5570,
                        'username', 'password')
```

```Lua
> conn = swat.CAS('cas.mycompany.com', 5570, 'username', 'password')
```

Java is a strongly typed programming language. In Java, you need to declare and create a new **CASClientInterface** object as a connection to the CAS server.

```Java
CASClientInterface conn = new CASClient('cas.mycompany.com', 5570,
                             'username', 'password');
```

The techniques above always create a new CAS session in the CAS server. A CAS session is an isolated execution environment that starts a session process on every machine in the cluster where the CAS server is deployed. All data sets that you upload to CAS stay local to that session unless you promote it to a global scope where it can be visible to other sessions in the server. This design enables multiple users to connect to the same computing cluster with resource tracking and management on the individual sessions. If something goes wrong in your session or the session dies, the CAS server and other sessions connected to the server are not affected.

A CAS session has its own identity and authentication. If you are authenticated, you can specify the session ID to reconnect to an existing CAS session.

```Python
In [3]: conn = swat.CAS('cas.mycompany.com',5570, 'username',
                        'password', session='sessionId')
```

```Lua
> conn = swat.CAS('cas.mycompany.com', 5570, 'username', 'password',
                  {session='sessionId'})
```

```JAVA
CASClient client = new CASClient();
client.setHost('cas.mycompany.com');
client.setPort(5570);
client.setUserName('username');
client.setPassword('password');
client.setSessionID('session-Id');
CASClientInterface conn = new CASClient(client);
```

CAS also includes an embedded web server that hosts the CAS Server Monitor web application. The web application provides a graphical user interface for monitoring the CAS server and the user sessions. If you open the server monitor, you can see how many client side connections have been established to a single CAS session (client count):

2

	UUID	User	Provider	Name	State	Idle Time	Action Count	Last Action	Client Count	
☐	c3fa4e78-5ea9-234a-adac-194ae343083f	ximeng	Active Directory	py-session-4 Mon Feb 27 15:55:23 2017	connected	00:03	20	session sessionname	4	⋮

CALLING CAS ACTIONS

A CAS server has both analytic and basic operational action sets. Each action set contains one or more actions. In Python or Lua, you can call a CAS action as a method on the CAS connection object that we created in the previous section. For example, you can call the **actionsetInfo** action to print out the action sets that have been loaded into the server.

Python
```
In [4]: conn.actionsetInfo()
```

Lua
```
> conn:actionsetInfo()
```

Action Output
```
Action set information

             actionset                     label  loaded   extension  \
    0     accessControl      Access Controls       1      tkacon
    1     accessControl      Access Controls       1      casmeta
    2          builtins             Builtins       1    tkcasablt
    3     configuration    Server Properties       1     tkcascfg
    4    dataPreprocess      Data Preprocess       1      tktrans
    5          dataStep            DATA Step       1     datastep
    6        percentile           Percentile       1     tkcasptl
    7            search               Search       1       casidx
    8           session      Session Methods       1     tkcsessn
    9       sessionProp   Session Properties       1     tkcstate
    10           simple     Simple Analytics       1     tkimstat
    11            table               Tables       1     tkcastab

              build_time                portdate  product_name
    0    2017-02-26 20:16:29   V.03.02M0P02262017          tkcas
    1    2017-02-26 20:16:29   V.03.02M0P02262017          tkcas
    2    2017-02-26 20:16:30   V.03.02M0P02262017          tkcas
    3    2017-02-26 20:16:27   V.03.02M0P02262017          tkcas
    4    2017-02-26 20:16:29   V.03.02M0P02262017        crsstat
    5    2017-02-26 20:15:59   V.03.02M0P02262017          tkcas
    6    2017-02-26 20:16:29   V.03.02M0P02262017        crsstat
    7    2017-02-26 19:52:11   V.03.02M0P02262017      crssearch
    8    2017-02-26 20:16:29   V.03.02M0P02262017          tkcas
    9    2017-02-26 20:16:29   V.03.02M0P02262017          tkcas
    10   2017-02-26 20:16:29   V.03.02M0P02262017        crsstat
    11   2017-02-26 20:16:29   V.03.02M0P02262017          tkcas
```

In Java, you need to invoke an action using the client side **Invoke** method. You also need to explicitly declare the action object (**action1**) and the action result object (**results**). The Java output is skipped because it is identical to the Python/Lua output above.

Java
```
ActionSetInfoOptions action1 = new ActionSetInfoOptions();
CASActionResults<CASValue> results = null;
```

```
try {
    results = client.invoke(action1);
} catch (CASException e) {
    // handle CAS exception here
} catch (IOException ioe){
    // handle other exception here
}
for (int i = 0; i < results.getResultsCount(); i++) {
    System.out.println(results.getResult(i));
}
```

There are several alternative ways to submit CAS actions in Java. For example, you can get the same action result in a fluent programming manner.

```
results = client.getActionSets().builtins().actionSetInfo().invoke();
```

The **help** action is probably the most frequently used CAS action in the beginning. You can use the **help** action to list the actions available in a specific CAS action set, or print the parameter descriptions of a specific action. The following example shows how to use this action to display the actions in the **table** action set, and the parameters of the **tableInfo** action.

Python
```
In [5]: conn.help(actionset='table')
```

Lua
```
> conn:help{actionset='table'}
```

Java
```
HelpOptions help = client.getActionSets().builtins().help();
help.setActionSet('table');
CASActionResults<CASValue> results = help.invoke();
```

Action Output

	name	description
0	view	Creates a view from files or tables
1	attribute	Manages extended table attributes
2	upload	Transfers binary data to the server ...
3	loadTable	Loads a table from a caslib's data s...
4	tableExists	Checks whether a table has been loaded
5	columnInfo	Shows column information
6	fetch	Fetches rows from a table or view
7	save	Saves a table to a caslib's data source
8	addTable	Add a table by sending it from the c...
9	tableInfo	Shows information about a table
10	tableDetails	Get detailed information about a table
11	dropTable	Drops a table
12	deleteSource	Delete a table or file from a caslib...
13	fileInfo	Lists the files in a caslib's data s...
14	promote	Promote a table to global scope
15	addCaslib	Adds a new caslib to enable access t...
16	dropCaslib	Drops a caslib
17	caslibInfo	Shows caslib information
18	queryCaslib	Checks whether a caslib exists
19	partition	Partitions a table
20	shuffle	Randomly shuffles a table
21	recordCount	Shows the number of rows in a Cloud ...

```
   22   loadDataSource   Loads one or more data source interf...
   23        update                Updates rows in a table
```

Python
```
In [6]: conn.help(action='tableInfo')
```

Lua
```
> conn:help{action='tableInfo'}
```

Java
```
HelpOptions help = client.getActionSets().builtins().help();
help.setAction('table');
CASActionResults<CASValue> results = help.invoke();
```

Action Output
```
NOTE: Information for action 'table.tableInfo':
NOTE: The following parameters are accepted.  Default values are
shown.
NOTE:    string name=NULL (alias: table),
NOTE:         specifies the table name.
NOTE:    string caslib=NULL,
NOTE:         specifies the caslib containing the table that you want
to use with the action. By default, the active caslib is used.
Specify a value only if you need to access a table from a different
caslib.
NOTE:    boolean quiet=false (alias: silent)
NOTE:         when set to True, attempting to show information for a
table that does not exist returns an OK status and severity. When set
to False, attempting to show information for a table that does not
exist returns an error.
```

When you start a new CAS server, several CAS action sets are preloaded. Except for the **simple** action set, these action sets are mainly for basic operational functionality such as server setup, authentication and authorization, session management, and table operations. To use other action sets available in your CAS server, you need to load them into your CAS session. In Python or Lua, you can load an action set on demand using the **loadActionSet** action. For example, let's load the regression action set that contains linear regression, logistic regression, and generalized linear models.

Python
```
In [7]: conn.loadActionset('regression')
```

Lua
```
> conn:loadActionset{actionset='regression'}
```

Java
```
client.loadActionSet(null, 'regression');
```

UNDERSTANDING CAS ACTION RESULTS

Similar to the ODS tables produced by SAS procedures, CAS actions also produce results that are downloaded to the client. Regardless of which programming interface you use to invoke the action, the information that is returned is the same. However, due to the different capabilities of each language, they are presented to you in different formats. In Python, the results of a CAS action call is actually a **CASResults** object, which is a subclass of the Python **OrderedDict** (a dictionary with keys that remain in the same order as were inserted).

```
Python
In [8]: result = conn.serverstatus()
   ...: type(result)
Out[8]: swat.cas.results.CASResults


In [9]: result.keys()
Out[9]: odict_keys(['About', 'server', 'nodestatus'])
```

We can look at an individual result from an action call using Python's key-value syntax. Unlike SAS ODS tables, the results from CAS action might not always to be a structured table. In the above example, the **About** result is a dictionary, and the other two results (**server**, **nodestatus**) are tabular output. In Python, such results are stored as a **SASDataFrame**, which is a sub-class of the famous Pandas **DataFrame**.

```
Python
In [10]: for key in result:
   ...:      print('Type of ' + key + ' is ' +
                     type(result[key]).__name__)

Type of About is dict
Type of server is SASDataFrame
Type of nodestatus is SASDataFrame
```

A **SASDataFrame** is equivalent to a Pandas **DataFrame** for client side operation. It simply contains extra metadata about the table and columns such as labels, formats, and so on. You can work with a **SASDataFrame** just like working with a Pandas **DataFrame**:

```
Python
In [11]: result['nodestatus'].head(2)
Out[11]:
Node Status

                    name      role      uptime    running   stalled
0   cas02.mycompany.com     worker    9718.606          0         0
1   cas03.mycompany.com     worker    9718.605          0         0
```

In Lua, the collection of results from a CAS action is simply a Lua table. Each result in the collection is a Lua table as well.

```
Lua
> result = conn:serverstatus{}
> type(result)
table

> for key, value in pairs(result) do
>>      print('Type of ' .. key .. ' is ' .. type(value))
>> end
Type of server is table
Type of About is table
Type of nodestatus is table
```

In Java, the collection of results from a CAS action is a **CASResults** object. You use the **getResultsCount** and **getResult** methods to loop through the collection and display each action result.

```
for (int i = 0; i < results.getResultsCount(); i++) {
    System.out.println(results.getResult(i));
}
```

WORKING WITH CAS ACTION RESULTS

If you connect to a CAS server and run a CAS-enabled procedure in a SAS environment, the results that you get are ODS tables. If you want to process the data within an ODS table, you first need to use ODS Output to convert the table into a SAS data set. It can then be processed using SAS procedures or DATA step. In Python or Lua, you can work with the result tables using the native methods that are available for a Pandas DataFrame or a Lua table.

First, let's run the **tableInfo** action to see how many data sets have been loaded into the CAS server.

```
Python
In[12]: result = conn.tableInfo()
   ...: df = result['TableInfo']
   ...: df
```

```
Lua
> result = conn:tableInfo()
> tbl = result['TableInfo']
```

```
Java
TableInfoOptions info1 = client.getActionSets().table().tableInfo();
CASActionResults<CASValue> results = info1.invoke();
```

```
Action Output
```

	Name	Rows	Columns	Encoding	CreateTimeFormatted	\
0	CARS	428	15	utf-8	27Feb2017:16:28:45	
1	ORGANICS	1688948	36	utf-8	27Feb2017:16:28:51	
2	ATTRITION	90831	14	utf-8	27Feb2017:16:32:23	

	ModTimeFormatted	JavaCharSet	CreateTime	ModTime	\
0	27Feb2017:16:28:45	UTF8	1.803832e+09	1.803832e+09	
1	27Feb2017:16:28:51	UTF8	1.803832e+09	1.803832e+09	
2	27Feb2017:16:32:23	UTF8	1.803832e+09	1.803832e+09	

	Global	Repeated	View	SourceName	SourceCaslib	Compressed	\
0	1	0	0			0	
1	1	0	0			0	
2	1	0	0			0	

	Creator	Modifier
0	sasdemo	
1	sasdemo	
2	sasdemo	

You can apply DataFrame methods on this output directly. For example, you can index or filter the table, or apply the **max** method on the Rows column to determine the maximum number of rows of all of the loaded tables.

```
Python
In [13]: resultTable[['Name', 'Rows', 'Columns']]
Out[13]:
```

	Name	Rows	Columns
0	CARS	428	15
1	ORGANICS	1688948	36
2	ATTRITION	90831	14

```
In [14]: df[df['Rows'] > 1000][['Name', 'Rows', 'Columns']]
Out[14]:
         Name     Rows  Columns
1   ORGANICS  1688948       36
2  ATTRITION    90831       14

In [15]: df['Rows'].max()
Out[15]: 1688948
```

The counterpart of Pandas DataFrame in Lua is the Lua table object. The Lua **SWAT** package extends the table object by adding new behaviors to handle the tabular output from CAS actions. For example, you can print out the first row of the **TableInfo** result as follows.

```
Lua
> tbl[1]

{["Name"]="CARS", ["Rows"]=428, ["Columns"]=15, ["Encoding"]="utf-8",
["CreateTimeFormatted"]="27Feb2017:16:28:45",
["ModTimeFormatted"]="27Feb2017:16:28:45", ["JavaCharSet"]="UTF8",
["CreateTime"]=1803832125.8, ["ModTime"]=1803832125.8, ["Global"]=1,
["Repeated"]=0, ["View"]=0, ["SourceName"]="", ["SourceCaslib"]="",
["Compressed"]=0, ["Creator"]="sasdemo", ["Modifier"]=""}
```

The **SWAT** package also provides fancy indexing. You can select a subset of rows, or columns, or both.

```
Lua
> tbl{'Name','Rows','Columns'}

Table Information for Caslib CASUSERHDFS(ximeng)
Name           Rows  Columns
CARS            428       15
ORGANICS    1688948       36
ATTRITION     90831       14

> tbl{1,3}{'Name','Rows','Columns'}

Table Information for Caslib CASUSERHDFS(ximeng)
Name         Rows  Columns
CARS          428       15
ATTRITION   90831       14
```

In Java, all action results are wrapped as a **CASValue** object, which is simply a key-value pair. Similar to the action results returned to the Python or Lua client, the action results in Java could be either tabular or non-tabular format. The Java client also provide a few useful methods to work with tabular action outputs. For example, you can obtain the column names and row counts using the **getColumnNames** and the **getRowCount** methods.

```
Java
TableInfoOptions info1 = client.getActionSets().table().tableInfo();
CASActionResults<CASValue> results = info1.invoke();
CASTable tbl = (CASTable) results.getResult(0).getValue();
System.out.println(tbl);
System.out.println(tbl.getColumnNames());
System.out.println(tbl.getRowCount());

Java Output
```

```
[Name, Rows, Columns, Encoding, CreateTimeFormatted,
ModTimeFormatted, JavaCharSet, CreateTime, ModTime, Global, Repeated,
View, SourceName, SourceCaslib, Compressed, Creator, Modifier]
3
```

You can fetch a row or a cell from a tabular CAS action output as well.

Java
```
System.out.println(tbl.getRow(1));
System.out.println(tbl.getStringAt(1,"Name"));
System.out.println(tbl.getIntAt(1,"Rows"));
```

Java Output
```
[ORGANICS, 1688948, 36, utf-8, 03Mar2017:20:26:09,
03Mar2017:20:26:09, UTF8, 1.80419196925421E9, 1.80419196925421E9, 1,
0, 0, null, null, 0, ximeng, null]
ORGANICS
1688948
```

EXPLORING YOUR DATA

Before we can do any sort of statistical analyses, we need to look at the data to better understand it. CAS provides the **simple** action set that contains data exploration and data summary actions for operations such as computing summary statistics, topK, or distinct counts, one-way or two-way frequency tables, and so on. Let's first try to print some univariate statistics from the attrition table.

Python
```
In [16]: conn.summary(table='cars')
```

Lua
```
> conn:summary{table='cars'}
```

Java
```
SummaryOptions summary1 = client.getActionSets().simple().summary();
Castable castable = new Castable();
castable.setName("cars");
summary1.setTable(castable);
CASActionResults<CASValue> results = summary1.invoke();
```

Action Output
```
 Descriptive Statistics for CARS
```

	Column	Min	Max	N	NMiss	Mean \
0	MSRP	10280.0	192465.0	428.0	0.0	32774.855140
1	Invoice	9875.0	173560.0	428.0	0.0	30014.700935
2	EngineSize	1.3	8.3	428.0	0.0	3.196729
3	Cylinders	3.0	12.0	426.0	2.0	5.807512
4	Horsepower	73.0	500.0	428.0	0.0	215.885514
5	MPG_City	10.0	60.0	428.0	0.0	20.060748
6	MPG_Highway	12.0	66.0	428.0	0.0	26.843458
7	Weight	1850.0	7190.0	428.0	0.0	3577.953271
8	Wheelbase	89.0	144.0	428.0	0.0	108.154206
9	Length	143.0	238.0	428.0	0.0	186.362150

	Sum	Std	StdErr	Var	USS \
0	14027638.0	19431.716674	939.267478	3.775916e+08	6.209854e+11
1	12846292.0	17642.117750	852.763949	3.112443e+08	5.184789e+11

2	1368.2	1.108595	0.053586	1.228982e+00	4.898540e+03
3	2474.0	1.558443	0.075507	2.428743e+00	1.540000e+04
4	92399.0	71.836032	3.472326	5.160415e+03	2.215110e+07
5	8586.0	5.238218	0.253199	2.743892e+01	1.839580e+05
6	11489.0	5.741201	0.277511	3.296139e+01	3.224790e+05
7	1531364.0	758.983215	36.686838	5.760555e+05	5.725125e+09
8	46290.0	8.311813	0.401767	6.908624e+01	5.035958e+06
9	79763.0	14.357991	0.694020	2.061519e+02	1.495283e+07

	CSS	CV	TValue	ProbT
0	1.612316e+11	59.288490	34.894059	4.160412e-127
1	1.329013e+11	58.778256	35.196963	2.684398e-128
2	5.247754e+02	34.679034	59.656105	3.133745e-209
3	1.032216e+03	26.834946	76.913766	1.515569e-251
4	2.203497e+06	33.275059	62.173176	4.185344e-216
5	1.171642e+04	26.111777	79.229235	1.866284e-257
6	1.407451e+04	21.387709	96.729204	1.665621e-292
7	2.459757e+08	21.212776	97.526890	5.812547e-294
8	2.949982e+04	7.685150	269.196577	0.000000e+00
9	8.802687e+04	7.704349	268.525733	0.000000e+00

In both Python and Lua, you can define a **CASTable** object that references the CAS table in the server. You can then submit CAS actions on the **CASTable** object as if they are methods on the object.

```
Python
In [17]: cars = conn.CASTable('cars')
    ...: cars.summary()


Lua
> cars = conn:CASTable{name:'cars'}
> cars:summary{}
```

Although the **CASTable** object in Python is just a reference to the actual CAS table which does not live in the Python environment, you can still treat it like a **DataFrame** and apply **DataFrame** methods on the CASTable object, such as **groupby**.

```
Python
In [18]: cars.groupby('origin').summary(subset=['min','max'])
Out[18]:
[ByGroupInfo]

ByGroupInfo
```

	Origin	Origin_f	_key_
0	Asia	Asia	Asia
1	Europe	Europe	Europe
2	USA	USA	USA

```
[ByGroup1.Summary]

Descriptive Statistics for CARS
```

Origin	Column	Min	Max
Asia	MSRP	10280.0	89765.0
Asia	Invoice	9875.0	79978.0
Asia	EngineSize	1.3	5.6
Asia	Cylinders	3.0	8.0

```
Asia       Horsepower      73.0     340.0
Asia         MPG_City      13.0      60.0
Asia      MPG_Highway      17.0      66.0
Asia           Weight    1850.0    5590.0
Asia        Wheelbase      89.0     140.0
Asia           Length     153.0     224.0
```

```
[ByGroup2.Summary]

Descriptive Statistics for CARS

                 Column       Min        Max
Origin
Europe             MSRP   16999.0   192465.0
Europe          Invoice   15437.0   173560.0
Europe       EngineSize       1.6        6.0
Europe        Cylinders       4.0       12.0
Europe       Horsepower     100.0      493.0
Europe         MPG_City      12.0       38.0
Europe      MPG_Highway      14.0       46.0
Europe           Weight    2524.0     5423.0
Europe        Wheelbase      93.0      123.0
Europe           Length     143.0      204.0
```

```
[ByGroup3.Summary]

Descriptive Statistics for CARS

                 Column       Min        Max
Origin
USA                MSRP   10995.0    81795.0
USA             Invoice   10319.0    74451.0
USA          EngineSize       1.6        8.3
USA           Cylinders       4.0       10.0
USA          Horsepower     103.0      500.0
USA            MPG_City      10.0       29.0
USA         MPG_Highway      12.0       37.0
USA              Weight    2348.0     7190.0
USA           Wheelbase      93.0      144.0
USA              Length     150.0      238.0
```

This is equivalent to the following.

```
In [19]: cars.set_param('groupby','origin')
   ...: cars.summary(subset=['min','max'])
```

In contrast, in both Lua and Java, you need to specify the **groupby** variable as a parameter to the table.

Lua
```
> cars2 = conn:CASTable{name='cars',groupby={'origin'}}
> cars2:summary{subset={'min','max'}}
```

Java
```
SummaryOptions summary1 = client.getActionSets().simple().summary();
// define the input CAS table
Castable castable = new Castable();
castable.setName('cars');
```

11

```
// define the group by variable
Casinvardesc groupbyVar = new Casinvardesc();
groupbyVar.setName("Origin");
castable.setGroupBy(new Casinvardesc[] {groupbyVar});

// define the statistics to compute
summary1.setSubSet(new SummaryOptions.SUBSET[]
                          {SummaryOptions.SUBSET.MIN,
                           SummaryOptions.SUBSET.MAX});

summary1.setTable(castable);
SummaryOptions summary1 = client.getActionSets().simple().summary();
CASActionResults<CASValue> results = summary1.invoke();
```

BUILDING ANALYTIC MODELS

CAS provide a variety of statistical models and machine learning models. These models are grouped into action sets based on functionality. For example, the **regression** action set contains several regression models such as linear regression, logistic regression, and generalized linear models. Let us continue to use the **cars** data and build a simple logistic regression model to predict the origin of the vehicles.

Python
```
In [20]: cars.logistic(
    ...:      target = 'Origin',
    ...:      inputs = ['MSRP', 'MPG_CITY']
    ...: )
```

Lua
```
> cars:logistic{target='Origin',inputs={'MSRP','MPG_City'}}
```

Java
```
LogisticOptions logit1 =
client.getActionSets().regression().logistic();

// define the input CAS table;
Castable castable = new Castable();
castable.setName("cars");
logit1.setTable(castable);

// define the input variable list;
Casinvardesc var1 = new Casinvardesc();
var1.setName("MSRP");
Casinvardesc var2 = new Casinvardesc();
var2.setName("MPG_City");
logit1.setInputs(new Casinvardesc[] {var1, var2});

// define the target variable;
String target = "Origin";
logit1.setTarget(target);

CASActionResults<CASValue> results = logit1.invoke();
```

Action Output
```
 Model Information

           RowId                 Description  \
```

```
0          DATA                    Data Source
1    RESPONSEVAR           Response Variable
2       NLEVELS   Number of Response Levels
3          DIST                 Distribution
4      LINKTYPE                    Link Type
5          LINK                Link Function
6          TECH      Optimization Technique


                                  Value
0                                 CARS
1                               Origin
2                                    3
3                          Multinomial
4                           Cumulative
5                                Logit
6   Newton-Raphson with Ridging
```

[NObs]

Number of Observations

```
     RowId                     Description  Value
0    NREAD   Number of Observations Read    428.0
1    NUSED   Number of Observations Used    428.0
```

[ResponseProfile]

Response Profile

```
     OrderedValue Outcome  Origin   Freq
0               1    Asia    Asia  158.0
1               2  Europe  Europe  123.0
2               3     USA     USA  147.0
```

[ConvergenceStatus]

Convergence Status

```
                                    Reason  Status   MaxGradient
0   Convergence criterion (GCONV=1E-8) s...      0   7.492139e-08
```

[Dimensions]

Dimensions

```
           RowId                  Description  Value
0    NDESIGNCOLS           Columns in Design      4
1       NEFFECTS           Number of Effects      3
2      MAXEFCOLS           Max Effect Columns     2
3     DESIGNRANK               Rank of Design      4
4        OPTPARM   Parameters in Optimization      4
```

[GlobalTest]

Testing Global Null Hypothesis: BETA=0

```
                Test  DF     ChiSq     ProbChiSq
```

```
0  Likelihood Ratio   2  31.881151  1.194252e-07
```

[FitStatistics]

Fit Statistics

```
   RowId                  Description        Value
0  M2LL           -2 Log Likelihood    903.963742
1  AIC           AIC (smaller is better)   911.963742
2  AICC          AICC (smaller is better)  912.058305
3  SBC           SBC (smaller is better)   928.200235
```

[ParameterEstimates]

Parameter Estimates

```
       Effect   Parameter            ParmName Outcome  Origin  DF  \
0  Intercept   Intercept      Intercept_Asia    Asia    Asia   1
1  Intercept   Intercept    Intercept_Europe  Europe  Europe   1
2       MSRP        MSRP                MSRP                    1
3    MPG_City    MPG_City            MPG_City                   1
```

```
    Estimate     StdErr       ChiSq      ProbChiSq
0  -3.367872   0.658085   26.190709   3.093071e-07
1  -2.116690   0.646503   10.719456   1.060148e-03
2   0.000006   0.000005    1.698431   1.924932e-01
3   0.130489   0.027169   23.067706   1.563956e-06
```

[Timing]

Task Timing

```
              RowId                Task      Time     RelTime
0            SETUP   Setup and Parsing  0.044817   0.104601
1     LEVELIZATION         Levelization  0.022141   0.051676
2   INITIALIZATION  Model Initialization  0.000426   0.000994
3             SSCP     SSCP Computation  0.002401   0.005604
4          FITTING        Model Fitting  0.110876   0.258781
5           OUTPUT  Creating Output Data  0.237345   0.553955
6          CLEANUP              Cleanup  0.002248   0.005247
7            TOTAL                Total  0.428455   1.000000
```

REST INTERFACE

CAS also provides a REST API interface for your web applications to monitor CAS server status and execute CAS actions directly. The REST endpoints are organized into three categories:

- /cas - Information about the CAS server, session creation and action submission.
- /system - Information about the system running CAS.
- /grid - Information about a cluster running CAS.

To get the nodes of the cluster running CAS, you can use the **/cas/nodes** endpoint.

```
GET cas.mycompany.com:[port]/cas/nodes
```

To submit a CAS action, you can post to **/cas/actions/[action name].** The following example shows how to submit a **summary** CAS action on the cars table to obtain the summary statistics for the MSRP values of the vehicles.

```
POST cas.mycompany.com:[port]/cas/actions/summary?table=cars&inputs=MSRP
```

To specify more action parameters such as a list of input variables, you need to add `Content-Type: application/json` in the header and pass your parameters in JSON format in the body of your REST call. The following postman screenshots show how to submit a summary action to compute the minimum and maximum values of MPG_City and MPG_Highway columns.

SUPPORTED VERSIONS

- 64-bit Lua 5.2 or later. Install the middleclass (4.0+), csv, and ee5_base64 Lua packages.
- 64-bit Python 2.7.x or 3.4.x
- Java 8 or later

CONCLUSION

This paper provides an introduction to the three programming interfaces to SAS® Cloud Analytic Services (CAS): Python, Lua, and Java. For more information about these CAS clients, you can visit the Viya documentation site for more information. http://support.sas.com/documentation/onlinedoc/viya/index.html

RECOMMENDED READING

- *SAS® Viya – The Python Perspective*

CONTACT INFORMATION

Your comments and questions are valued and encouraged. Contact the authors at:

Xiangxiang Meng, PhD
SAS Institute, Inc.
Xiangxiang.Meng@sas.com

Kevin D Smith
SAS Institute, Inc.
Kevin.Smith@sas.com

Check out these related books in the SAS® bookstore:

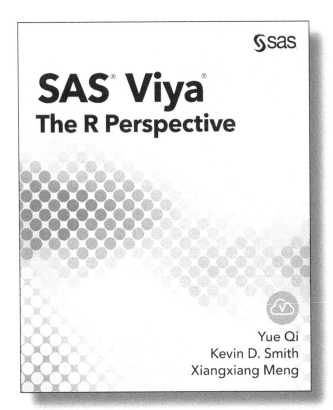

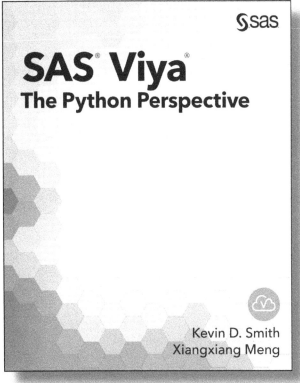

For 20% off these e-books, visit **sas.com\books** and use the code WITHSAS20

sas.com/books
for additional books and resources.

THE POWER TO KNOW®

www.ingramcontent.com/pod-product-compliance
Lightning Source LLC
Chambersburg PA
CBHW060111090326
40690CB00064B/5113